£4.50
US $8.95
CAN $11.20

CONTENTS

FEATURES

5 : THE UNKNOWN FOREST
As *Doctor Who* celebrates thirty years of time travelling, Marcus Hearn looks back at the various ways in which the programme has been perceived by its more high-brow viewers.

21: CROSSWORD
A Thirtieth Anniversary puzzle compiled by Nigel Robinson, the author of Target Books' *The Doctor Who Crossword Book*.

35: WHOFAX
Andrew Pixley has compiled a list of who, when and how many – the ultimate *Doctor Who* trivia listing!

43: DOCTOR WHO?
Tim Quinn and Dicky Howett take a look back over thirty years of *Doctor Who*!

49: THIRTY YEARS OF FICTION
A year-by-year guide to events in the Doctor's life.

55: THIRTY YEARS OF FACT
A year-by-year guide to events in *Doctor Who*'s transmission.

61: CROSSWORD ANSWERS
The solution, plus another dip into the Thirtieth Anniversary celebrations by Tim Quinn and Dicky Howett.

FICTION

8: A RELIGIOUS EXPERIENCE
The First Doctor visits a planet where he and Ian Chesterton are hailed as gods. But all is not well in paradise. A new comic strip adventure by **Tim Quinn, illustrated by John Ridgway**.

16: LOOP THE LOUP
The Second Doctor bites off more than he can chew when a distressed shepherd cries wolf . . . A new story by Marc Platt, author of *The New Adventures – Time's Crucible* Illustrated by Paul Vyse.

22: RECONNAISSANCE
The Third Doctor leaves Liz Shaw in the lurch while he visits the committee responsible for funding UNIT. While he's away, Liz meets a strange man and comes to an important decision . . . A new story by Terrance Dicks, author of *The New Adventures – Exodus* and illustrated by Phil Bevan.

27: REST AND RE-CREATION
The Fourth Doctor and Leela are planning a quiet picnic but two aggressive Zygons interrupt their day! A new comic strip by Warwick Gray, with artwork by Charlie Adlard.

38: THE CHANGELING YEARS
The Fourth Doctor and Leela encounter a strange city where a controlled experiment in time manipulation is taking place... A new story by Gareth Roberts, author of *The New Adventures – The Highest Science* and illustrated by Paul Vyse.

44: PERFECT DAY
The Fifth Doctor and Tegan Jovanka take a trip to Earth's future, just in time to say farewell. A new story by Mark Gatiss, author of *The New Adventures – Nightshade* and illustrated by David Miller.

50: THE MORE THINGS CHANGE
A young soldier remembers The Sixth Doctor and Peri and the effect they have had on his life. A new story by Andy Lane, co-author of *The New Adventures – Lucifer Rising* and illustrated by Phil Bevan.

56: PULLING STRINGS
A strange time experiment has an important effect on the lives of the Seventh Doctor and Melanie Bush. A new story by Nigel Robinson, author of *The New Adventures – Birthright* and illustrated by Brian Hudd.

Doctor Who Yearbook™ 1994. Published by Marvel Comics UK Ltd. Jim Galton, Chairman. Vincent Conran, Managing Director. Office of publication 13/15 Arundel Street, London WC2R 3DX, England. Published annually. All Doctor Who material is © BBC TV 1993. Diamond Logo © BBC Enterprises 1973. Thirtieth Anniversary Logo © BBC Enterprises 1993. All other material is © Marvel Comics Ltd unless otherwise indicated. The Doctor Who Yearbook™ 1994 - created by the busy team of gnomes called Gary Russell, Marcus Hearn, Perl Godbold, Gary Knight, Louise Cassell, Julie Pickering, Chris McCormack, Mathew Hyde, Fiona Moscatelli and Paul Neary. No similarity between any of the fictional names, characters, persons and/or institutions herein with those of any living or dead persons or institutions is intended and any such similarity is purely coincidental. Nothing may be reproduced by any means in whole or part without the written permission of the publishers. This periodical may not be sold, except by authorised dealers, And is sold to the condition that it shall not be sold or distributed with any part of its cover or markings removed, nor in a mutilated condition. Printed in Italy

THE UNKNOWN FOREST

Photo © BBC Video

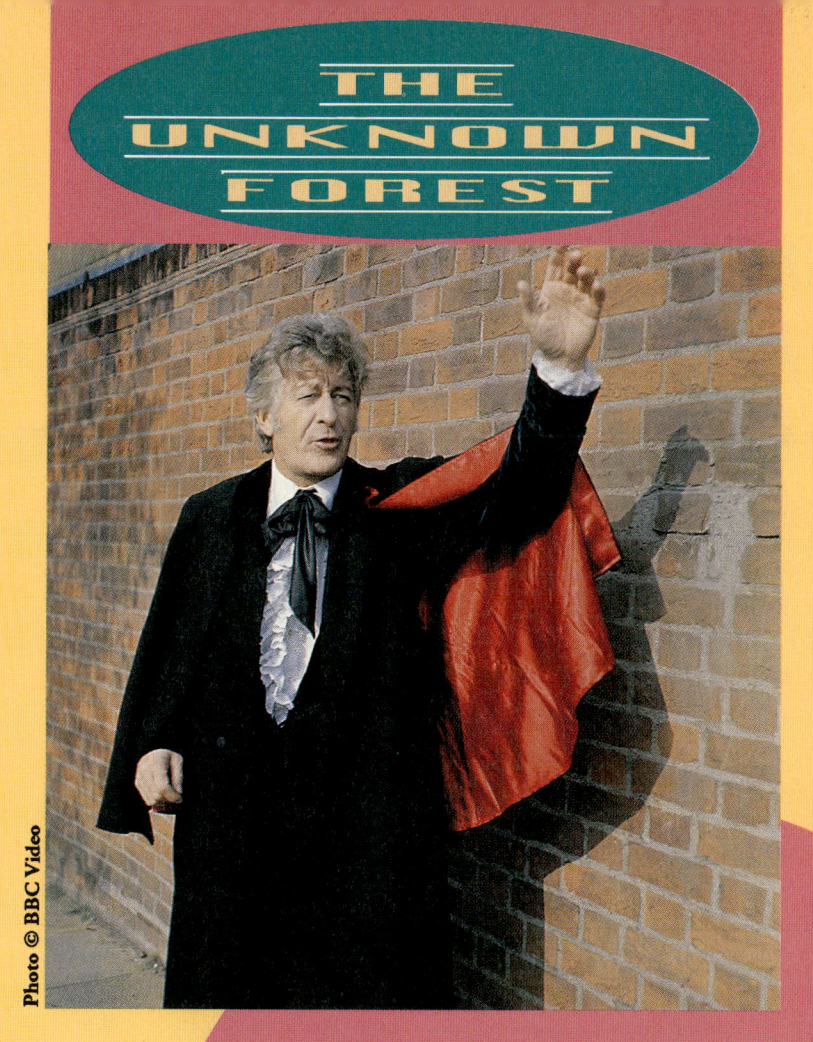

Doctor Who enthusiasts share an unspoken acceptance of the programme's enduring appeal. But how have others defined it? Marcus Hearn chairs a debate between TV arts presenter Melvyn Bragg, The Socialist Workers' Party, and a Dalek . . .

From a safe distance of thirty years it's easy to take the success of *Doctor Who* for granted. Generations of youngsters and adults have had their imaginations elasticated by the adventures of an alien man in a flying telephone box, and many have ventured plausible suggestions as to why.

Sir Huw Wheldon, the former managing director of the BBC, believed the programme was about "something archetypal . . . the path into the unknown forest," whereas in 1969 *The New Statesman* simply summarised the series as "the all-time Daddy's electric train."

WHAT IT IS

Interpretations of the programme's appeal are as numerous and varied as theories explaining what it is actually about, but in 1977 Melvyn Bragg stated something nobody could argue with: "*Doctor Who* has become one of the great characters of modern fiction, like Tarzan or Billy Bunter. And if you think that's easy to do, as Frank Richards said in a letter to George Orwell, you just try to make a character as popular and as realisable."

The gauntlet was picked up by Sydney Newman, the BBC's Head of Drama, in 1963. "*Doctor Who* was really the culmination of almost all my interests in life," he later admitted. "I wanted to reflect contemporary society; I was curious about the outer space stuff; and also, of course, being a children's programme, it had to have a high educational content. Up to the age of forty, I don't think there was a science-fiction book I hadn't read. I love them because they are a marvellous way – and a safe way, I might add – of saying nasty things about our own society. I love the satirisation and the extension of the present world – showing how it might be, given slightly different circumstances. My basic passion is the world today: how it is and how it might be changed, where it ought to be changed . . . "

He noted his original ideas on to a few pages and a national institution was born. "I'd give a million bucks if I could find that memo!" he now laments.

"Looking back, I suppose *Doctor Who* taught me the sheer wonder of fantasy," reflected the late Innes Lloyd, one of *Doctor Who*'s first producers, "and that science-fiction had far more potential as a storytelling device than I ever anticipated. You could easily cover all manner of tragedy and drama and still include light-hearted moments, and even comedy for certain elements. Some people I met at the time had a very pompous attitude towards watching the programme, but I'm sure that the adults were tempted at the odd moment to join their children behind the couch."

So what is *Doctor Who* actually about? According to telefantasy writer Christopher Penfold, the BBC don't know themselves. "The BBC has never really understood science-fiction," he once complained. "I think *Doctor Who* is something they've handled forever without ever really understanding."

Mary Tamm, who played the Fourth Doctor's companion Romana, was in no confusion when asked about the series. "The basic principle of the programme is quite simple: the Doctor is the hero of the piece, the girl asks the questions, a few monsters are the bad guys, and there are loads of corridors to run down. It's worked like that for a long time and there is no reason why it should not continue in that simple format because that is what the audience likes. They like the comfort of knowing exactly what they are going to get. And they like stories they can follow relatively easily. That is why programmes like *Star Trek* and *Coronation Street* have been so popular. They don't go too far out of the little sphere of activity which the audience expects."

WHAT IT ISNT

The Socialist Workers' Party magazine, *Socialist Review*, expressed no such favourable comparisons with Captain Kirk and his crew. In a 1984 article entitled 'Mao and the Time Lords', they offered their own manifesto for the show's success. "The BBC has provided the world with a popular Maoist sci-fi interpretation of the struggle for national liberation and revolution. It is a classic Maoist ▶

Mary Tamm, who played the first Romana, believes that Doctor Who had just a few basic principles.
Photo © BBC.

Peter Davison remembers being asked about his philosophy of Doctor Who - reading the scripts was his answer! Photo © BBC Video.

make a daft programme like that! It's utterly British in its concept and quirkiness, the eccentricity, devotion to characters rather than action."

Jean Marsh, an actress with the honour of appearing in some of the show's earliest and last episodes, said: "I think it's successful because people want to have crushes on other people. To have a crush on a slightly comic old British TV series is not so weird."

Maybe not, but how would you cope if *you* suddenly found a hall full of people who had a crush on you?

"I remember the first convention I ever did," recalled a disturbed Peter Davison. "They asked my philosophy of *Doctor Who* and I said 'I get the script and learn the words,' and they thought that was an awful thing to say. They do care about it, as I did when I was doing it myself, but at the same time you have to laugh at it too, or it gets very po-faced."

"A school of thought exists which holds the Daleks to be the sole master-key on the ring of clues to the popularity of *Doctor Who*," claimed *The Evening Standard* in 1977. "Admittedly the viewers fall for anything and everything – Emus, Michael Crawford, Starsky, or is it Hutch? But none match the intensity of the national love affair with these callous tyrants, gliding round their antiseptic control rooms and hiding, as all tyrants hide, a pathetic piece of humanoid debris under their armoured tops."

More often than not, it was actually Robert Jewell who was hiding under the armoured tops. The Dalek operator explained his own ideas behind the success of *Doctor Who* in 1987. "It's just like *The Mousetrap* that's played in the West End for so many years. It goes on and on and there's a new era and a new lot of people watching and then their children are watching. *Doctor Who* was really the first sci-fi programme to really hit the air-waves – *Lost in Space* and *Star Trek* all followed on. It has also been the kind of programme where writers have always been able to find something to write about. They can let their imaginations go and bring in so many different aspects, so many variations to stories, and its all accepted because that's what *Doctor Who* is."

WHAT ITS APPEAL IS...

"*Doctor Who* appealed to me because in fantasy you can use all these other elements and discuss any political, philosophic or psychological idea which if you keep hidden adds to the story enormously," cited Ian Stuart Black, reinforcing the idea and explaining his motivation for writing for the show in the Sixties. "When I analyse it I can see why it's so popular and has lasted all this time. The trick with the show is that it has this capacity for constant change. It has a

◀ text for national liberation. Power comes from the jet of a Dalek arm. Though *Doctor Who* is a product of the upturn in struggle of the Sixties and Seventies, the show remains in the elitist traditions of bourgeois revolution. The oppressed and exploited creatures who *Doctor Who* leads time after time to victory never have any control over the Vanguard Party (the Doctor and his friends) who are in all senses of the word alien to them. The victory of progressive forces is an alliance of all classes in which class differences are masked and hidden. The victory leads to restoration of the status quo before the imperialists arrived, not to worker's control. Workers' councils are not set up. The Doctor never educates the workers to their rôle as the ruling class of the post-revolutionary world. But, in spite of these criticisms the series is pro-revolt and anti-imperialist and a million light years more progressive than *Star Trek*."

Some of the monsters are quite good too. One of them, chief Ice Warrior and *Carry On* star Bernard Bresslaw, reckoned the show's lasting appeal stemmed from its early monochrome adventures. "I happen to believe there are certain disadvantages to the colour episodes of today. I do like science-fiction and I cannot help thinking that some of the best science-fiction films have been in black and white . . . That is the secret of good science-fiction: imagination first, technicalities second."

Wendy Padbury, who journeyed with Patrick Troughton's Doctor, felt that "being in black and white then added to its charm. When you see some of those old programmes that they bring out from twenty-five years ago in black and white, some of them hold up really well. I don't know how *Doctor Who* holds up because we're living in a more technical age, but I really like the black and white stories."

Unfortunately, one woman's quaint nostalgia is another man's old hat. "*Doctor Who* is too parochial, too amateur by Nineties standards," believes director Lovett Bickford, who worked on the programme in 1980. "I think it already was, when I did it, to an extent. It wasn't slick enough, it wasn't realistic enough and it wasn't frightening enough. *Doctor Who* is a bit Sixties and it was very good in the early days but, technically, we're so much more sophisticated than we've ever been that it would have to come up to that standard. *Doctor Who* just wasn't good enough in the end. It was becoming, sadly, too pantomimic when it should have been becoming more serious and more frightening. Science-fiction is wonderfully exciting but it should not be costume drama."

Two people responsible for making the show when it's popularity was at its highest have gone on record saying it's the cosy home-grown air which sustained popularity. "*Who* was very 'British science-fiction' and that was one of its great charms," says writer David Fisher. The show's producer in the late Seventies, Graham Williams, was also prone to a spot of flag-waving. "It doesn't compromise. It doesn't try and be American. It doesn't try and be anything except what it is. It is just uniquely British. I can't think of any other country in the world who would neat framework and to be truthful it isn't always *Doctor Who* is it? It's called *Doctor Who* but it can be anything within the basic premise of humanity moving through time and space. It's a smart cookie's set up!"

"That's quite a nice angle to explore," concurs *Doctor Who* novelist and actor David Banks, "as long as it doesn't get in the way of a good adventure so that children of six can hide behind the sofa, and students can write dissertations about it!"

Victor Pemberton, who never wrote any dissertations but wrote generally perceived good *Doctor Who* scripts, felt the same way. "I've always felt very deeply about the world and I think *Doctor Who* is very important for that. I know Verity Lambert, who first produced *Doctor Who*, was very keen to bring this element out. It's television with a conscience, a moral – although I don't think a TV is there to lecture people. If there's a message, fine, and if a writer feels strongly enough, fine – but *Doctor Who* is entertainment with a capital 'E' and that, I think, is why it has survived for so long."

Doctor Who's entertainment value was really recognised by the public with the advent of the Daleks and later the Cybermen, so maybe they're responsible for the show's longevity? Not according to occasional guest star Frank Windsor, whose personal preference was for historical stories. "Although the Daleks and the Cybermen are probably the strongest single memories for people who have watched *Doctor Who*, if it had been just that, would it have lasted as long as it has?"

The late Dennis Spooner, who wrote a few of the early historical tales, quite naturally felt the same way. "I don't think that if we had only done science-fiction in the early years that *Doctor Who* would have become the success it has."

Perhaps one of the most common reasons cited for the programme's success is its popularity with children, who apparently quite enjoy it too.

"There is this fear of the term children's programme," claimed Matthew Waterhouse, who played the Fourth and Fifth Doctor's youthful chum Adric. "Everyone used to think the Daleks were great, loads of adults who grew up with it still watch it. It's a very important part of children's culture, so how could anybody say it's a snobby put-down to state that loads of kids love it? Great children's works – Beatrix Potter, Lewis Carroll – all live on for adults."

Verity Lambert, the show's original producer and midwife to a national institution, modestly attributed the success of her baby to the country's fathers. "A great reason for the programme's continuing success has to be the fact that every four or five years you have a new generation of kids growing up."

One of her writers, William Emms, also believed *Doctor Who* was an hereditary condition. "I think most of us were aiming at children from seven to seventy. I think it's lasted because it's lived on in a lot of people's imaginations and possibly a lot of people have transmitted it to their children."

"Why has the programme proved such a continuing success?" Patrick Troughton asked. "I think the simple answer to that is because new children keep being born!"

Writing of Troughton's Doctor in 1967, *The Times* suggested that: "*Doctor Who* is the most successful of children's programmes because it has matched its science-fiction setting with good story-telling, and the most ingenious array of props and electronic sound effects. The children can identify, too, with *Doctor Who*'s child companions. But most important of all, *Doctor Who*'s infallibility is a device that allows even a nervous child to believe that, in spite of the most alarming experiences, all will be well in the end. It is reality, or what passes for it, that children find truly terrifying."

Whatever the reasons behind *Doctor Who*'s success, the only obvious thing is that nobody over the last thirty years has been able to agree upon is what *Doctor Who* is. Maybe the answer lies in something that everybody enjoys about the programme, whatever medium it appears in. Something that may well have outlasted the television show itself...

"It's magic isn't it?" believes script writer Peter Ling. "They somehow managed to make magic respectable to modern, technologically-minded children. They couldn't really lose because they combined all the things children were interested in – aspects of space exploration combined with magic and making the impossible possible. Styles and fashions may change but storytelling is timeless – it will go on.

"The stories are the essence."

The late Patrick Troughton was considered infallible by *The Times* in 1967. Photo BBC Video.

Matthew Waterhouse likens *Doctor Who* to other great works of fiction for children, well-loved by adults, including Beatrix Potter and Lewis Carroll. Photo © BBC Video.

THE PLANET *SEETAR* IN THE MALACHI SYSTEM. PREVIOUSLY UNEXPLORED BY SPACE OR *TIME-TRAVELLERS* —

— UNTIL TODAY.

INCREDIBLE. IT'S ABSOLUTELY INCREDIBLE, DOCTOR!

REALLY, CHESTERTON? THE PLANET *QUINNUS* IN THE FOURTH UNIVERSE HAS TWICE THE INDIGENOUS LIFE FORMS *AND* A PURPLE SEA...

a religious experience.

STORY: TIM QUINN. ART: JOHN RIDGEWAY. LETTERS: JANEY RUTTER. COLOURS: CHRISSIE McCORMACK. EDITOR: JOHN FREEMAN.

...PERHAPS IF WE'D LANDED DURING THE DAYTIME, I MIGHT FIND THE PLACE MORE IMPRESSIVE.

OH DON'T BE SUCH A *MISERY*, DOCTOR. AS A BOY I USED TO DREAM OF PLACES LIKE THIS. ALL THOSE WORLDS I READ ABOUT IN BURROUGH'S *CARTER OF MARS* BOOKS...

TO THINK I'VE NOW TRAVELLED FURTHER THAN EVEN *HE* COULD IMAGINE!

IT'S NOT THE LIFE AND DEATH BATTLES WITH *DALEKS* OR *SARACENS* I'LL REMEMBER OF OUR TIMES TOGETHER—

—BUT QUIET MOMENTS LIKE THIS, ON SOME UNCHARTED *ALIEN PARADISE.*

HMMF! YES QUITE, MY BOY.

8

HOONA
I'M AFRAID I'VE NEVER HAD TOO MUCH TIME FOR SUCH BACKWARD PLANETS. BUT SUSAN WOULD HAVE LOVED THIS PLACE.
I STILL WONDER IF I MADE THE RIGHT DECISION, LEAVING HER BEHIND ON A PLANET DECIMATED BY DALEKS*.
* THE DOCTOR'S GRAND-DAUGHTER LEFT THE TARDIS IN THE DALEK INVASION OF EARTH - JOHN.
IT WAS NEVER MY INTENTION TO ABANDON HER, YOU KNOW. I WONDER HOW SHE THINKS OF ME NOW?
YOU DID THE RIGHT THING AND I'M SURE SHE'S HAPPY WITH THAT CAMPBELL FELLOW. PERHAPS YOU'LL MEET HER AGAIN SOMEDAY.
HOONA
DON'T TORMENT YOURSELF, DOCTOR. HELLO — LOOKS LIKE WE'VE GOT SOME COMPANY...
WONDER WHAT THEY'RE SO EXCITED ABOUT?
CHAP IN FRONT LOOKS LIKE SOME SORT OF HIGH PRIEST...
HOONA!
HOONA!
AIEEEE!
DOCTOR! WHAT IS IT?
HOLD ON, CHESTERTON!
RUMBLE
RRRR

SSSSSSS

KRAASH

"Are you all right, Doctor?"

"I've had better days. Let's get away from here!"

"I don't think that's going to be easy—"

"—and I don't think we can expect much help from the locals!"

"Just keep QUIET, Chesterton — and we may escape this monster!"

SSSSSK

GAAAAGH!

EEEEE

AEEK?

"Good! It doesn't like the torches — but we've got to rescue that poor fellow! What's that AWFUL noise it's making?"

"Some sort of sonar, I expect. Hmm..."

10

11

SOON—
STOP WORRYING, CHESTERTON. THE GIRLS WILL BE PERFECTLY ALL RIGHT IN THE TARDIS. I'M MUCH MORE INTERESTED IN THESE PEOPLE—
—AND THEIR DEVELOPING CULTURE.
I DON'T REGARD WORSHIPPING A MURDEROUS WORM AS THE SORT OF CULTURAL DEVELOPMENT I'D LIKE TO ENCOURAGE...
—AND, AS TASTY AS IT IS, I THINK ALL THIS FOOD COULD BE BETTER USED THAN BEING OFFERED TO US, DOCTOR.
REALLY? I THINK IT'S RATHER GOOD OF THEM TO HONOUR US LIKE THIS.
I THINK WE'RE ABOUT TO REPLACE THAT WORM AS THE LOCALS' GOD. AT LEAST WE WILL IF THE LOCAL WITCH DOCTOR ALLOWS IT!
WELL, WHERE'S THE HARM IN THAT? THE PRIMITIVE MIND OFTEN REACTS IN HUMBLE AWE TO ITS VERY SURROUNDINGS, SEEING THE MAJESTY IN ALL.
EVEN THE SIMPLEST OF THINGS CAN TAKE ON MYSTICAL PROPORTIONS.

PURELY ON INTELLECT ALONE, ARE WE NOT *GODS* TO THESE SIMPLE PRIMITIVE FOLK, HMM..? —MY GOODNESS!

KRASH!

BUT DOCTOR! MY POINT IS THAT WE'RE *NOT* GODS!

WORDS, WORDS! THESE PEOPLE WILL REVERE EITHER SOMEONE OR SOMETHING, WHATEVER WE SAY- IT'S IN THEIR NATURE!

WE'RE HARDLY TAKING ADVANTAGE OF THE SITUATION...

WHY YOU, POMPOUS OLD—

HEY, I THINK WE'RE EXPECTED TO TAKE ANOTHER LITTLE WALK, DOCTOR.

WHAT? OH VERY WELL, IF WE MUST...

HOONA! HOONA!

BACK AT THE SEASHORE—

DEAR ME, WHAT ARE THEY DOING WITH THAT YOUNG WOMAN?

DOCTOR— REMEMBER THE AZTECS? THE *HUMAN SACRIFICES*?

OF COURSE, MY BOY. I'M NOT SO OLD THAT I FORGET THINGS LIKE *THAT* YOU KNOW!

OH MY GOODNESS— YOU DON'T THINK...

I'M AFRAID I *DO*!

13

THEY THINK WE'VE DESTROYED THEIR OLD GOD — AND NOW THEY'RE PAYING HOMAGE TO THEIR NEW ONE — US!

AND I'M NOT GOING TO STAND FOR IT!

I'VE MET YOUR SORT BEFORE, CHUM — AND I WASN'T IMPRESSED THE FIRST TIME.

KRAK!

SPLENDID, MY BOY, SPLENDID. BUT I REALLY THINK WE SHOULD BE GOING — BEFORE EVENTS HAVE AN OPPORTUNITY TO TAKE A TURN FOR THE WORSE...

HURR?

DO YOU REALLY THINK YOUR ACTION HAS HAD THE SLIGHTEST EFFECT ON THESE PEOPLE?

ADMIRABLE SENTIMENTS MY BOY, BUT THESE PEOPLE ARE STILL VERY PRIMITIVE, SURELY YOU REALISE THAT? IT'S THEIR VERY INSTINCT TO MAKE THE UNKNOWN AN OBJECT OF WORSHIP...

AAAH! BARBARA MY DEAR — YOU'RE AWAKE AT LAST, I SEE!

AFTER PAST EXPERIENCE, PROBABLY NOT — BUT IF THEY DO RETURN TO SACRIFICE, AT LEAST IT WON'T BE FOR MY SUPPOSED BENEFIT.

WHERE'S VICKI, MY DEAR? NOT OUTSIDE I HOPE.
NO-SHE'S SLEEPING. WHAT HAVE YOU TWO BEEN UP TO?
THE DOCTOR'S BEEN INDULGING IN HIS FAVOURITE HOBBY, BARBARA - LORDING IT OVER THE LOCAL POPULATION.
NOW, NOW CHESTERTON- WE DID NO LASTING HARM...
VWORP! VWORP!
YEARS LATER...
HOONA! HOONA!
VWORP! VWORP!
GOOD EVENING. I DO HOPE I'M INTRUDING...
I THINK IT'S TIME THIS CAME TO AN END...

Loop the Loup

By Marc Platt

Just a few more steady heaves, thought the Doctor.

The body seemed to grow in weight, the further up the mountain he dragged it. He gave another backward tug, caught his ankle on a fallen branch and sat down in a snowdrift. Not the first time he'd fallen over that day.

The wind was biting in again and his ankle, twisted in a cleft of the branch, refused to come free. It hurt excruciatingly. He plucked strands of lambswool from his shaggy fur coat, just along that tear that split one side from top to bottom.

To the South, distant grey clouds billowed up over what, far below, would one day be called Lake Garda. Flakes of fresh snow were already settling on his Beatle-cut mop of hair. Soon the snow would cover the wolf tracks further down the slopes. Left to its own devices, Time covered its traces. The future, Flinthair the shepherd's future, had a merciless chill to it.

Exasperated, the Doctor scrabbled with frozen fingers for the axe tucked inside the dead man's belt. The copper axehead that had no business to be copper in 3,300 BC, cut through the branch after only a few blows. That would serve the smug archaeologists right. The Copper Age was not curtailed precisely at a Thursday teatime in February because someone suddenly discovered a bronze teapot. Nature tried out its options at every opportunity. The sad example laying lifeless at his feet, might one day resolve some of that wretched neatness. Pigeonholes really annoyed the Doctor. He'd never met a tidy pigeon in any of his lives.

He slid the axe back under the belt and gripped the stiffening body under its arms. Just a few more heaves, he thought, and this business could be left for someone else to deal with in their own time. But this business had not been what he had expected...

The bleating had started at about midday. It came from outside the TARDIS, but all he saw on the scanner was snow driving in the latest blizzard. The plaintive cries were unlike the bleating he usually got from his companions, so he opened the ship's outer doors and looked out. Something about half his height barrelled in out of the whiteness, knocking him backwards. He struggled up, shaking snow off his outsized frock-coat, and followed the intruder into his ship.

The sheep stood facing him beyond the half-dismantled central console. It was horned, long-haired and rather rotund, its fleece already dripping with melting ice. It let out a deep prolonged baa.

"Hello," said the Doctor, warily.

Oh dear, oh dear. He was very particular about visitors in his ship. This one looked unruly, unpredictable and probably unhouse-trained too. On one flank, its wool was marked with a strange pronged design in dark blue dye. It must have come from the village he had seen by the lake, and there was no taking it back there now. Not in this weather.

"Baa," it reiterated and sat down in rather graceless fashion. When it turned away, the Doctor saw a deep gash on its haunch, which dribbled blood into its matted wool. He edged a few steps closer and the stupid brute struggled up in a vain attempt at a dash for safety. Its hooves scrabbled wildly on the smooth floor and it toppled heavily onto its side. It lay uselessly flailing its legs at him.

Muttering words of encouragement, he bent to examine the bloody gash. It was the nasty work of some predator, probably a wolf. Then he noticed the movement of contractions in the distended stomach.

"Oh no," he exclaimed aloud. "I'm a Doctor, not a vet!"

"Baa," complained the expectant ewe.

"Baa humbug," retorted the Doctor. He took his fur coat from the hatstand and draped it over the creature which, to his surprise, went quiet. Then he went to look for some towels and hot water. Lots of hot water, that was what was always called for on these occasions.

It took ten minutes to find a suitable bowl of water and some towels in the TARDIS's extra-thermal dissipater unit, which often doubled as an airing cupboard. When he re-entered the console room, the sheep was lying in a pool of blood. For a moment, he thought the worst, but then it raised its head and gave him an exhausted bleat.

Something moved under the coat. The Doctor lifted the hem gingerly and saw a tiny lamb suckling at its mothers teat.

"Oh, well done, Ewe-ridice!" he exclaimed, giving a little jig of delight, which nearly spilled his hot water bowl.

Ewe-ridice the sheep was either content to let him clean the jagged wound, or too exhausted to resist. He punched up a hay-flavoured nutrient bar from the TARDIS food machine and fed it to her square by square. Then he retrieved his coat, settled the mother and wobbly child onto an old setee from a storage cupboard and set off for the village.

The snow had stopped, but it was

freezing hard under the full moon's freezing silvery eye. The Doctor hurried down the mountain, cutting a straight path between the tall, black shapes of the pine forest. THE TARDIS had dumped itself on the upper slopes, its instruments dead to the world. He had wasted hours looking for the problem to no avail. All it needed, he suspected, was a good kick, but he wasn't sure where or with what. He went for a walk and discovered the village nearby. He preferred to avoid visiting such primitive settlements. The locals invariably mistook him for a magician or a deity or something generally taboo and pointed unpleasantly sharp spears at him while they asked awkward questions.

He paused by a rock that looked like a danish pastry in the moonlight. Something was following him. He had heard it crunching through the snow. It stopped too. He walked on further and the crunching began again. In front of him, a line of pugmarks crossed his path. Further on was a second set, much larger with a pronounced lengthening of the claws. One foot dragged with a limp. He saw a dark shape darting between the darkness of the trees. A pair of hungry eyes caught the moonshine and regarded him from the shadows. He heard its soft growl.

Then, from the other direction, came a long baleful howl. The eyes vanished and he heard their owner bound away through the snow. He shuddered and wished he had waited until daybreak.

He had observed the village by the lake on the previous day, painstakingly staying within the edge of the forest to avoid causing a disturbance. It was a small archetypal farming and hunting community. But its squat, dark-haired occupants would never understand that they fitted into a neat Neolithic pigeonhole. They were too busy in the arduous task of survival. On the whole, he thought they were winning. He had seen fishing coracles on the lake and there were signs that the land had been tilled for crops, but the onset of the snow had put pay to that for the year.

The paling eastern sky was heavy with snow, but no fires burned in the village. The clustered houses teetered high on piles over the lake's marshy bank. The Doctor decided that the best approach was to walk in openly, but there were no guards to be seen. It was uncomfortably quiet. The stockade gate hung open.

He walked warily in, moving freely among the houses. He climbed ladders to peer into deserted rooms where the snow had blown in. He stared at the empty sheep fold. He examined the spilled contents of a half-full grain store. A brace of coracles lay overturned above the shoreline. A clay-lined cooking pit was still warm. On the track leading along the lake, he accidentally trod on a corn dolly that lay in the trampled slush. The place had been abandoned and they had left in a hurry. But no-one runs from a snowstorm.

At one end of the village was a mound of stones like a makeshift long barrow where the dead might be buried. The singularly unpleasant totem that stood beside it made the Doctor shudder. A human skull had been skewered onto a wooden pole. Crowning it like a headdress was the head of a wolf, fangs bared, with its body skin falling down behind. The Doctor could make an easy stab at the type of evil spirit it was meant to ward off.

He eyed his surroundings, uncomfortably certain that he was being watched. The freezing air had not bothered him before, but now he suddenly felt very cold inside.

Something snapped close by and he instinctively ducked. An arrow thunked into the totem an inch from his head. It had spiral feathers to make it spin in flight. The Doctor ran, scampering for cover between the raised piles of the houses until he fell headlong into the cooking pit and stayed crouching there.

By luck or some more iniquitous design of the cosmos, it had started to snow again. The Doctor could hear his hunter muttering as he searched. The voice was quietly on the edge of tears, sounding snatches of words like someone talking to his own lost soul. "He's there . . . seen him . . . the brute killed them . . . killed the others. Know he's there . . . saw him watching yesterday . . . Great wolf . . . slinking in the tree shadows. I'll kill him . . . where is he . . . then the rest'll come back . . . and I'll be back too . . . "

The Doctor sank lower into the pit. Was this possible? Had the villagers seen him and deserted their homes because they thought he was a killer? Worse, if he interpreted the totem's meaning correctly, they thought he was some sort of *Loupgarou*. A Lycanthrope. The Wolf that is Were. He shuddered in his fur coat. No, no, that wouldn't do at all. He doubted such a biological anomaly was possible. There was probably a large timber wolf lurking out there in the forest, frightening the locals. He may well have crossed its path already, and it terrified him too. The immediate prospect was no less worrying – an argument along the length of a flint-headed arrow, and he heard the hunter coming closer.

There was a sudden canine snarl and a man cried out in anguish. Snow was blowing into the Doctor's face, obscuring and view of the fight. He heard the cries and snarls fading into the blizzard and hauled himself out of the pit intent on following. The tracks led out of the village – a man and a wolf heading back up the mountain. They were soon obscured by fresh snow, leaving the Doctor alone, vulnerable and without direction. All he wanted was the safety of his TARDIS. Then he remembered the sheep that had taken up residence with him.

He ploughed on up the slope with snow caking into his hair and coat. He topped the danish pastry ridge and faltered. A body lay ahead in a drift. It was twisted and grey, the corpse of a large wolf. And its throat had been torn out.

As the Doctor bent over the wolf, he heard the snow scrunch at his back. A hand dragged him back and a flint blade pressed at his throat.

"Skin you alive, wolf demon," hissed the man's voice.

The Doctor nearly choked. "What a very silly idea," he said with as much authority as he could muster. "Do I look like a wolf man?"

The blade pressed tighter.

He tried to nod towards the wolf. "I wanted to help, but you've obviously solved the problem yourself. That was very clever. Well done!" He glanced down and saw that his assailant's arm was bore the same blue mark that he had seen on the sheep. "Look, I'll prove I'm not dangerous. I have a . . . *hut* further up where I've been sheltering one of your flock."

The arm jerked the Doctor round and he was face to face with the wildest visage he could ever remember. Madness lived in those eyes. The face was bloody and the coarse hair was stone grey.

"Show me . . . demon," he growled.

The Doctor fumbled for the TARDIS key. "You'll see," he said as they approached the police box. "I've never ever attacked anyone unprovoked." But the presence at his shoulder remained a menacing one. A shepherd called Flinthair, watching his every move, who'd seen the dried blood on his coat. The man wore deer skins and limped on an arthritic leg. On his back was a great carved bow. A shepherd, but a hunter too.

The snow that had drifted against the TARDIS, had been kicked away by the door. To the Doctor's annoyance, the cold had frozen the deadlock and it was ajar. He ushered Flinthair inside where the snow had blown in and waited for the usual reaction to the ship's dimensional riddle. He collided with the shepherd, who was backing out again, a look of horror on his face.

Blood had run into pools on the console room floor. The savaged remains of the unfortunate sheep and its lamb lay in the corner behind the settee, where their executioner had tried to hide its shameful butchery.

Death was the Doctor's constant companion. But this was his own ship, his sanctuary. He stared nervously at every corner of the console room. Now his home had been violated by an act of ferocious brutality and he, even he, floundered for words.

"Mr Flinthair, you must understand that I am as shocked as you. There is something more dangerous and unnatural at large than I imagined. We must take every step to seek it out very quickly."

He waited for the accusations, but the shepherd only stood, swinging his head back and forth like a dazed animal, as if trying to shake the jagged event neatly into his consciousness. He staggered forward, unable to take his eyes from the horror. Then he fell and the Doctor caught him,

19

pulling him back to rest against the wall. The wind was blowing in, and since they were clearly the only two living beings in the ship, the Doctor closed the doors. As they clunked shut, the shepherd spoke.

"A wolf demon attacked me in the woods, that was a moon ago. I killed it, but the spirit is tied to the earth. It didn't go. Then it killed my brother. He caught it taking our best ram. The demon tried to hide his body, but I found him and carried him home to the village." His voice cracked as he stared at the dead sheep. "They blamed me. They forced me out. The wise man cursed me and they drove me away." His face was smeared with blood that he had tried to wash away with snow. He dribbled. "So now I hunt the Great wolf again. And I shall drive it from the world."

The Doctor touched his shoulder gently. "And I shall help you." Flinthair's hands were frostbitten and dried blood clung under the unusually long nails. He turned slowly and said, "Demons are things of the past. I don't believe in them. They're in my head. One day there won't be any more demons."

The Doctor nodded grimly and slowly withdrew his hand. Flinthair's brown eyes had glinted with a depth of amber. It was all a matter of perspective. The villagers no more knew they were Neolithic than Flinthair knew what he was. Sometimes he was a man, sometimes he might be a wolf.

The shepherd tensed and his eyes glazed. "Demon? Have I found you?"

The Doctor backed away. "Perhaps," he said. "It may be closer than you think." The shepherd rose, but he had a stoop and his hands, more like claws now, were close to the floor.

"I should warn you that my ship is in a state of grace that prohibits acts of violence." The Doctor nearly tripped over the discarded body of the sheep.

Flinthair's mouth drew back into a snarl full of lengthening canines. Thick hair was darkening across his face as the two circled each other round the inoperative central console. The Doctor made a lunge for the door lever, but a mass of claws slashed across him. There was nowhere to run to. The shepherd no longer even remotely resembled a man. He was a bizarre hybrid, like a fairground grotesque dressed in ill-fitting clothes, spitting and snarling his hatred.

"That's not very wolf-like at all," huffed the circling Doctor. "Wolves are highly advanced creatures, with their own laws and social orders. Look!" He fished a mirror from his pocket and levelled it at the brute. "Just think what your family would say!"

Beyond such thoughts or memories, the creature sprang onto the top of the console and clambered over the glass cylinder of the Time Rotor towards him. Cables and loose instruments cascaded down. The Doctor slipped in the sheep's blood and fell. His arms flailed out, desperately grasping for some sort of defensive weapon. Above him, the monster crouched on the Time Rotor and howled at the ceiling.

There was a hum of power. The instruments inside the Rotor cylinder began to turn. This was just the kick-start the TARDIS had needed . . . albeit too late. The Time Rotor began to rise and the startled wolf-man half jumped, half fell onto the instrument panels below. There was a flash of silver. A fierce discharge of trapped artron energy from the ship's power house, arched upwards and earthed itself in a spirit still tied to the earth. The body was hurled towards the Doctor who flung up his arms for protection.

He heard a yelp of pain as the flint-headed arrow he had unwittingly seized, impaled itself in the shepherd's chest. Flinthair lay lifeless on top of the Doctor, a shepherd once again, if indeed he had ever been anything else. Perception, ably assisted by deception, had its own tricks to perform. The bodies of two dead sheep were the only testimony to what the shepherd had thought he was or wasn't, or what the Doctor, sometimes taken for a magician himself, imagined he had seen. Sleight of head. And what you could imagine, ladies and gentlemen, is often more powerful than truth.

You had a regard for the future, Mr Flinthair. You foresaw a time when demons would be banished and beliefs would be challenged. You can help with that. With luck they'll find you one day, trapped in ice like a fly in amber, ready to put a few perceptions about your time to flight. Just over the ridge by the danish pastry rock. You'll be sheltered there in an icepool, away from the slow torrential flow of the new glacier. Caught in that you'd be lost forever, carried down the mountain, no more than deep frozen wolf food. He'd seen it once in the papers, or thought he had. Thank you for starting my ship Mr Flinthair. Just a few more heaves and then you can rest in peace . . . for a while, that is.

CROSSWORD

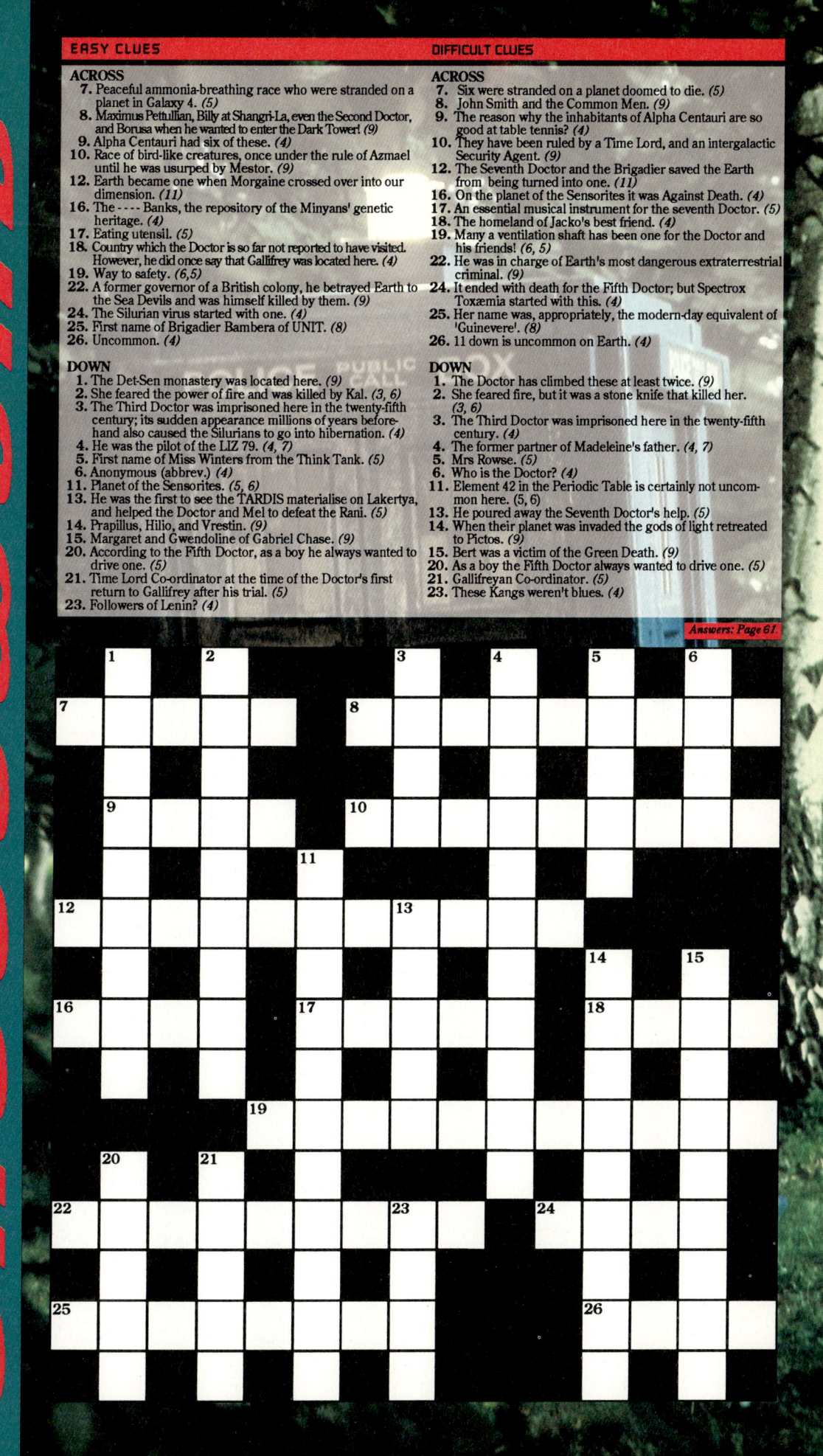

EASY CLUES

ACROSS
7. Peaceful ammonia-breathing race who were stranded on a planet in Galaxy 4. *(5)*
8. Maximus Pettullian, Billy at Shangri-La, even the Second Doctor, and Borusa when he wanted to enter the Dark Tower! *(9)*
9. Alpha Centauri had six of these. *(4)*
10. Race of bird-like creatures, once under the rule of Azmael until he was usurped by Mestor. *(9)*
12. Earth became one when Morgaine crossed over into our dimension. *(11)*
16. The - - - - Banks, the repository of the Minyans' genetic heritage. *(4)*
17. Eating utensil. *(5)*
18. Country which the Doctor is so far not reported to have visited. However, he did once say that Gallifrey was located here. *(4)*
19. Way to safety. *(6,5)*
22. A former governor of a British colony, he betrayed Earth to the Sea Devils and was himself killed by them. *(9)*
24. The Silurian virus started with one. *(4)*
25. First name of Brigadier Bambera of UNIT. *(8)*
26. Uncommon. *(4)*

DOWN
1. The Det-Sen monastery was located here. *(9)*
2. She feared the power of fire and was killed by Kal. *(3, 6)*
3. The Third Doctor was imprisoned here in the twenty-fifth century; its sudden appearance millions of years beforehand also caused the Silurians to go into hibernation. *(4)*
4. He was the pilot of the LIZ 79. *(4, 7)*
5. First name of Miss Winters from the Think Tank. *(5)*
6. Anonymous (abbrev.) *(4)*
11. Planet of the Sensorites. *(5, 6)*
13. He was the first to see the TARDIS materialise on Lakertya, and helped the Doctor and Mel to defeat the Rani. *(5)*
14. Prapillus, Hilio, and Vrestin. *(9)*
15. Margaret and Gwendoline of Gabriel Chase. *(9)*
20. According to the Fifth Doctor, as a boy he always wanted to drive one. *(5)*
21. Time Lord Co-ordinator at the time of the Doctor's first return to Gallifrey after his trial. *(5)*
23. Followers of Lenin? *(4)*

DIFFICULT CLUES

ACROSS
7. Six were stranded on a planet doomed to die. *(5)*
8. John Smith and the Common Men. *(9)*
9. The reason why the inhabitants of Alpha Centauri are so good at table tennis? *(4)*
10. They have been ruled by a Time Lord, and an intergalactic Security Agent. *(9)*
12. The Seventh Doctor and the Brigadier saved the Earth from being turned into one. *(11)*
16. On the planet of the Sensorites it was Against Death. *(4)*
17. An essential musical instrument for the seventh Doctor. *(5)*
18. The homeland of Jacko's best friend. *(4)*
19. Many a ventilation shaft has been one for the Doctor and his friends! *(6, 5)*
22. He was in charge of Earth's most dangerous extraterrestrial criminal. *(9)*
24. It ended with death for the Fifth Doctor; but Spectrox Toxæmia started with this. *(4)*
25. Her name was, appropriately, the modern-day equivalent of 'Guinevere'. *(8)*
26. 11 down is uncommon on Earth. *(4)*

DOWN
1. The Doctor has climbed these at least twice. *(9)*
2. She feared fire, but it was a stone knife that killed her. *(3, 6)*
3. The Third Doctor was imprisoned here in the twenty-fifth century. *(4)*
4. The former partner of Madeleine's father. *(4, 7)*
5. Mrs Rowse. *(5)*
6. Who is the Doctor? *(4)*
11. Element 42 in the Periodic Table is certainly not uncommon here. *(5, 6)*
13. He poured away the Seventh Doctor's help. *(5)*
14. When their planet was invaded the gods of light retreated to Pictos. *(9)*
15. Bert was a victim of the Green Death. *(9)*
20. As a boy the Fifth Doctor always wanted to drive one. *(5)*
21. Gallifreyan Co-ordinator. *(5)*
23. These Kangs weren't blues. *(4)*

Answers: Page 61.

Reconnaissance

By Terrance Dicks

"No, no no!" said the Doctor, sharply, tossing the sheaf of calculations aside. "My dear Liz, how many times must I explain? You've made an elementary error in the primary stages. Anyone with the remotest knowledge of temporal physics can see that."

Liz Shaw, who had quite a temper herself, slammed her hand down on the lab bench, rattling the test-tubes in their rack.

"My dear Doctor, how many times must I explain that I don't *have* the remotest knowledge of temporal physics? Always excepting your oh-so-brilliant self, I doubt if anybody on the planet has. You can't expect me to run before I can walk."

"Run, no," said the Doctor. "But surely one might hope for a few stumbling steps?"

Liz drew a deep breath. "Now listen Doctor What's-your-name, I offered to help you with those calculations out of the kindness of my heart. But you don't need anyone's help do you? You know it all! All you need is someone to pass you your test-tubes and tell you how wonderful you are!"

"Ha-herrum!"

Both combatants turned at the sound of ferocious throat-clearing from the lab doorway. There stood the immaculately-uniformed figure of Brigadier Alastair Lethbridge-Stewart.

"Ready, Doctor?"

"What do you want?"

Ignoring this ungracious reception, the Brigadier said "We're attending the Cabinet Security Committee this morning."

"*You* may be, Brigadier. I've got work to do."

Calmly the Brigadier went on, "The committee, I must remind you Doctor, is ultimately responsible for UNIT funding. And the size of the UNIT budget is directly linked to the amount of costly scientific equipment you need – most of which you seem to blow up with remarkable regularity."

"I still don't see –"

"If the Government are to continue funding UNIT, they need to be convinced of our usefulness. In other words, they need to know what we've been doing recently. You, Doctor, are uniquely qualified to tell them."

The Doctor had never been overburdened with modesty. "Yes, well I suppose I am. Very well Brigadier, don't dawdle, come along. We'll go through those calculations again later, Liz. Don't worry, you'll soon get the hang of it." The Doctor strode from the room.

"If you'll excuse us, Miss Shaw," said the Brigadier politely.

"Willingly," said Liz. Raising her voice she added, "and don't hurry back!"

The Brigadier winced, then turned and followed the Doctor.

He caught up with him in the UNIT car park, where the Doctor was already sitting at the wheel of his souped-up Edwardian roadster.

'We're attending a top-level Government Committee, Doctor."

"So?"

"I had thought – the UNIT limousine . . ."

"Don't be so status-conscious, Brigadier. Bessie will whizz us through the Westminster traffic in no time."

"That's what I'm afraid of . . ."

As they sped along the road towards Westminster the Brigadier said diplomatically, "Did I sense an atmosphere of tension in the lab just now, Doctor?"

"Oh you don't want to take any notice of that, Brigadier," said the Doctor, neatly cutting up an astonished taxi. "She's a good girl, Liz. Just a bit touchy that's all . . ."

The Brigadier raised an eyebrow. "Which reminds me . . . you'll be polite to the Cabinet Committee, won't you, Doctor?"

"Me, Brigadier? I'm the soul of tact, you know that. A born diplomat . . ."

In the laboratory, Liz Shaw threw down the sheaf of calculations in despair, still unable to see where she'd gone wrong. "Time I got out of this place," she grumbled to herself. "Never wanted to come here to start with . . ."

She thought back to her time as a research scientist in Cambridge, the sudden summons to a mysterious security organisation called UNIT and her first interview with the Brigadier.

She'd been suspicious from the very first, reluctant to believe the Brigadier's theory that the Earth was in danger from invasion from space. "We have drawn attention to ourselves, Miss Shaw," he'd said, and cunningly hooked her interest with a tale of a meteor shower that behaved in ways that were scientifically impossible.

Soon after that she'd met the Doctor . . .

It wasn't that the Doctor meant to be infuriating, thought Liz struggling to be fair. "He must be feel the way I'd feel if I had a toddler for my assistant," thought Liz. "Only here *I'm* the child, grappling with things I can't possibly understand."

Elizabeth Shaw came to a decision. She would resign from UNIT, go back to Cambridge, and resume the pursuit of knowledge in her own way and at her own speed . . .

Behind her a deep voice said, "Forgive me for disturbing you. I was looking for my old friend, the Doctor." Liz turned and saw a man standing in the doorway. For some strange reason he reminded Liz of the Doctor, although there was none of the Doctor's flamboyance about him. He was medium-sized, bearded, powerfully-built, and he wore severe-looking dark clothes with a high-collared jacket.

As he came into the room the stranger smiled, revealing an unexpected powerful charm. "They sent me here from reception," he said. "This is the Doctor's laboratory?"

"Yes it is, but I'm afraid you've just missed him. He's gone off to a conference with the Brigadier."

"May I ask when he'll be back?"

"No idea. But it's a government committee, I imagine they'll be there for quite some time."

"Dear oh dear, and I was so looking forward to meeting the Doctor again. He looked round the laboratory. "This is all very impressive. I gather the Doctor actually works here?"

23

"He's our Scientific Adviser."

"Well, well, well... You know, I never thought the Doctor would ever settle down to a regular job. He was always rather erratic as a student."

Liz looked thoughtfully at him. "Did you say you were an old friend of the Doctor?"

"We were at school together," said the stranger.

"I see. Well, if you can leave an address or a telephone number, I'm sure he'll get in touch with you." She thought for a moment. "Tell you what, why don't I give you the address of the Committee Rooms? Perhaps you could catch up with him there, meet him when he comes out."

"If it's not too much trouble."

"Not a bit, I've got it here somewhere..."

Liz went to her bag on the end of the bench and felt inside. When she straightened up and turned there was a small black automatic in her hand.

Liz had objected violently when the Brigadier issued her with the weapon, and sent her on a one-day training course in its use. But she was glad of it now. Remembering what she'd been taught she flipped the safety-catch with her thumb and worked the slide, pumping a round into the chamber.

"Raise both hands please, and step back." The stranger obeyed. He seemed more amused than alarmed.

"My dear young lady, there's no need for that!"

"No? Well, for your information, visitors to UNIT are always strictly escorted, not left to wander around alone. And I don't know much about the Doctor and where he comes from, but I very much doubt any of his old school-chums are likely to pop up here in London."

The stranger's voice was curiously soothing. "I can quite understand your suspicions, my dear, but there is really no reason to worry. You can see I am telling the truth. You have only to look at me..." The voice deepened into a tone of command. "Look at me! Look at me! Look at me!"

Liz looked into the dark burning eyes – and then of course it was all over. The Master took the gun from Liz's unresisting fingers, put the safety-catch back on and returned it to her bag. Like the hypnotised sentries at the gate, Liz was no danger to him now. The Master drew up a lab stool and rested his elbows on the bench. "Set down, my dear – and tell me *everything* you know about the Doctor." Liz began talking in a calm conversational voice. "I first saw the Doctor at Ashbridge Cottage Hospital...

"... and after that the Inferno project was closed down, and we returned to UNIT HQ," concluded Liz. "Since then the Doctor has been working on the calculations to re-program the dematerialisation circuit of his TARDIS. These calculations..."

The Master snapped his fingers. "Enough!" Immediately Liz fell silent. She had been talking non-stop for several hours.

The Master glanced at the square blue shape in the corner of the lab. "Poor Doctor! Exiled to Earth with an immobilised TARDIS. Who says the High Council has no sense of humour..."

He sat haunched on his stool, mulling over the immense amount of information Liz had given him during her hypnotically induced total recall of the Doctor's recent adventures. How could he best make use of all he had learned? The Nestene Consciousness sounded promising... So too did the Silurians, though the Brigadier, more realistic than the incorrigible do-gooder the Doctor, seemed to have disposed of them most effectively. Still, thought the Master, there might be some survivors. In the depths of the sea, perhaps... It was worth investigation. There was nothing for him in the business of the alien astronauts. They had been returned now, and it was too late to stir up further trouble. The Inferno project too was a thing of the past, a splendid disaster spoiled by the Doctor's meddling.

The Master's mind returned to the Nestene Consciousness. He had heard of it of course. The Master's knew of most forces for evil in the cosmos. A fiercely rapacious entity with its curious affinity for plastic. Savage and determined, not really of any great intelligence. But guided, controlled... There were distinct possibilities, especially at this particular stage of Earth's development.

The Master looked at the telephone on a table in the corner. He moved over to it, an the plastic cord through his fingers. He looked at the bunch of daffodils in a bowl on the window sill and smiled. Oh yes, he thought, distinct possibilities.

He moved back to the lab bench and stood looking thoughtfully at Liz Shaw, who sat wide-eyed and motionless on her stool. The Master fingered a stubby metallic device in his pocket. It might be amusing to leave a tiny shrunken corpse for the Doctor to find on his return. But then the Doctor would be forewarned. Such a pity to spoil the surprise of their coming reunion. It would be even more amusing to booby-trap the TARDIS, so that when the Doctor opened the door . . .

Amusing, but crude. Clumsy. Not artistic. After all, he could kill the Doctor any time. But to subjugate Earth to a blindly malignant force that the Doctor believed he had already defeated – and then kill him . . .

The Master snapped his fingers. "Listen to me, Miss Shaw. You have spent the day working on your calculations. No-one has disturbed you. I was never here."

"You were never here," said Liz. The Master snapped his fingers and Liz became absorbed in her calculations. If she could find where she went wrong . . .

The Master moved through the corridors of UNIT HQ protected by his cloak of hypnotic invisibility. As he strode through the main gates the sentries presented arms. Acknowledging the salute with a casual nod, the Master went on his way. He would need a base, he thought, somewhere to serve as his own headquarters, and, if necessary, as a trap. He remembered a huddle of tents on a little green not too far away. Perfect, thought the Master. The Doctor had always been fond of circuses. He should have a little amusement – before the end . . .

Happily absorbed in evil thoughts, the Master headed for his TARDIS, currently in the form of a news kiosk. There was nothing wrong with *his* chameleon circuit. Keen-eyed and vigilant, the UNIT sentries resumed their patrol. Someone enormously important had just left UNIT, though they weren't sure who . . .

Then they forgot all about him.

Her head filled with figures, Liz Shaw was disturbed by the sound of raised voices coming towards her down the corridor. "I don't care what you say, Doctor," said the Brigadier. "Making frequent use of such expressions as 'a motley crew of pompous bungling bureaucratic nincompoops' is *not* what I call being tactful with the Committee."

"What does it matter?" said the Doctor cheerfully. "They agreed to pay up, didn't they? Even increased your budget."

"Only because you threatened to re-activate the Autons, unearth more Silurians, call back the alien astronauts and re-start drilling on the Inferno project!"

"Well it worked, didn't it? Now, if you'll forgive me, Brigadier, I must make my peace with Miss Shaw."

Liz heard the Brigadier go into his office and close the door behind him. The Doctor came into the laboratory, looking as humble and penitent as he knew how. "Liz, do forgive me, I'm an impatient egotistical idiot. It's just that it's so important to me you see . . . " he broke off at the sight of her face. "Liz, what's the matter?" She rubbed her eyes. "Nothing . . . Wrestling with these figures has given me a bit of a headache . . . I seem to have picked up a sore throat as well."

The Doctor beamed, anxious to make amends. "No wonder you feel seedy. You've been stuck in here and I've been cooped up with a committee. Come on Liz, we need fresh air. Its still a nice afternoon, we'll go for a walk in the park."

As they strolled along the edge of the lake, picking their way between picnicking families, Liz said, "I've been thinking of going back to Cambridge, taking up my research again."

The Doctor looked shocked. "Not because of . . . "

Liz grinned and shook her head. "No,

25

I'm used to your little tantrums, they don't really bother me."

"I see," said the Doctor drily. "What then?"

"It's just that . . . Well, working with you Doctor reminds me of how much I have to learn. Somehow it's, well, discouraging . . ."

As they walked along, Liz had been watching a mother and child sitting on the grass just ahead. She touched the Doctor's arm. "Look, Doctor." They stopped and watched for a moment. The child was just at the staggering stage, walking a few steps, collapsing, struggling up again. When the mother tried to help, the child roared with rage and pulled away. It clambered to its feet and staggered a few more steps.

The Doctor nodded. "We all have to learn, don't we?"

"That's right," said Liz. "On our own."

Even as they watched, the child suddenly got the hang of the mysterious business of walking. Legs pumping hard, it shot away from its mother at amazing speed, heading straight for the lake. In a few long strides, the Doctor headed it off, scooped it up and returned the child to its mother, politely brushing aside her thanks.

As they resumed their walk, the Doctor glanced down at Liz. "Though of course sometimes . . ."

Liz smiled. "All right, Doctor. But I still think it's time I took my own steps – even if I have to fall in my own lake a few times!"

"Well, don't do anything in a hurry," said the Doctor. "And do forgive my impatience and rudeness earlier. You're a great help to me Liz. We're a good team, and I'd hate to lose you." Liz couldn't help feeling pleased. "I haven't really made my mind up, Doctor, not yet. I'm just thinking it over."

They were approaching the park gate now and the Doctor said apologetically, "I think I'll pop back to the lab, Liz. Those figures . . . Coming?"

Liz shook her head. "I've had enough for the day. See you in the morning."

As she watched his tall figure stride away, Liz realised that she really had made up her mind. She'd call Cambridge, not tomorrow maybe, but soon.

The Doctor paused by the gate and waved, and Liz waved back. She frowned, suddenly oppressed with the feeling that there was something important she had to tell him. The thought refused to formulate itself, disappearing behind some barrier in her mind. The feeling faded away. It couldn't have been anything very important, thought Liz.

She decided that when she did finally leave, she'd just go. She wouldn't even stop to say goodbye to the Doctor. Because if she did, he'd talk her out of going . . .

ANKTRA INHALES DEEPLY AND RECITES AN ANCIENT LITANY OF BLOOD AND FORTUNE..

—HIS EYES NEVER LEAVE HIS ENEMY.

KESTRAL RETURNS THE STARE. HE PUSHES BACK A SUDDEN WAVE OF HATRED AND CALMS HIS MIND.

HIS HAND SLOWLY BECOMES A FIST.

A BLOOD-FEUD IS TO BE SETTLED TODAY. THE ZYGON WARLORDS WILL FACE EACH OTHER IN RITUAL COMBAT...

—BUT NOT IN THEIR NATURAL STATE...

—THEIR BODIES ARE STUNTED AND CLUMSY. AS CUSTOM DEMANDS, THEY DISCARD THEM.

ENERGY FLOWS AND TRANSFUSES. MUSCLE TISSUE EXPANDS AND RESHAPES...

THEY ARE BORN ANEW.

Rest & re-creation

SCRIPT: WARWICK GRAY
ART: CHARLIE ADLARD
COLOURS: HELEN NALLY
LETTERS: JANEY RUTTER
EDITOR: GARY RUSSELL

ELSEWHERE...

"I'VE ALWAYS FELT *SHONTAA* TO BE A HIGHLY UNDER-RATED WORLD, LEELA... IT HAS A UNIQUE ETHER-EALITY, SUBTLY UNDERLINED BY ITS OWN STARK, BARREN AMBIENCE..."

"YES, DOCTOR. AND THERE ARE MANY *ROCKS* HERE AS WELL."

"YES, I NOTICED THAT TOO!"

"AH, NOW THAT'S INTERESTING..."

"A MAAKRIAN SWAMP-BEAR IS ATTEMPTING TO BITE THE HIND LEG OFF A TEKAZOID CAVE-BEAST."

"WHY IS THAT INTERESTING, DOCTOR?"

"WELL, FOR *ONE* THING, THE MAAKRIAN SWAMP-BEAR IS A PECULIAR SHADE OF *GREEN*... AND FOR *ANOTHER*, THE TWO SPECIES NORMALLY EXIST AT OPPOSITE ENDS OF THE GALAXY."

"AH... THINGS ARE BECOMING SLIGHTLY *CLEARER* NOW."

"*ZYGONS!*"

"SO, TWO ZYGONS *FIGHTING* EACH OTHER! A DUEL PERHAPS? YES, A *DUEL!*"

"YOU'D THINK THEY COULD FIND A MORE *DIGNIFIED* WAY TO SPEND AN AFTERNOON."

"HOW DO THEY CHANGE THEIR SHAPE?"

"I'LL EXPLAIN ON THE WAY. WE'RE GOING TO END THIS NONSENSE RIGHT NOW!"

"DOCTOR, IF THIS IS A DUEL OF HONOUR WE SHOULD NOT INTERFERE!"

"WHAT'S SO HONOURABLE ABOUT TWO REGRESSIVE SOCIO-PATHS HACKING EACH OTHER TO DEATH? BESIDES, THERE'S MORE AT STAKE HERE THAN THOSE TWO IDIOTS, LEELA..."

ANKTRA HAS DRAWN FIRST BLOOD. KESTRAL HAS SHIFTED INTO THE BODY OF A DOX BARBARIAN...

ANKTRA HAS FOLLOWED SUIT AS A SHAD'ATH GLADIATOR.

THERE IS AN UNDENIABLE EXHILARATION PRESENT IN THIS CLASH. THE WARLORDS' SENSES SUDDENLY SHARPEN AS ADRENALIN FLOWS THROUGH THEIR NEW FORMS.

THEY POSSESS BOTH GRACE AND POWER NOW. IT IS SO UNLIKE THEIR TRUE EXISTENCE.

ANKTRA FINDS HIMSELF STIFLING A GRIN AS HE FORCES KESTRAL BACK...

THIS IS THE ZYGON SPACECRAFT, DOCTOR?
YES, AND ONLY A *SCOUTING VESSEL*, TO BOOT. THEY MAY WELL HAVE COME HERE ALONE...
VZZZZ
THEN THERE WILL BE NO-ONE ELSE ON BOARD?
WELL NO OTHER *ZYGONS*, PERHAPS...
GOOD, NO SIGN OF LIFE—LEELA, I THINK WE'RE IN *LUCK* FOR A CHANGE!
RRRRR
THIS MUST BE THE RESIDENT *WATCHDOG*...
THE BEAST IS SAVAGE, DOCTOR!
YOU SHOULD MEET ITS LARGER COUSIN THE *SKARASEN* SOMETIME...

31

THE WARRIOR FORMS HAVE BEEN ABANDONED. ANKTRA IS NOW A *KORJAN* ANTHROPOID.

KESTRAL COUNTERS AS A *POLAR MODRELIAN.*

IT IS A MISTAKE. THE KORJAN'S REFLEXES ARE LIGHTNING SWIFT. KESTRAL FINDS HIS GREATER BULK AN IMMEDIATE HINDRANCE.

HE RETREATS, FRANTIC-ALLY SEARCHING FOR A SUITABLE SUBJECT WITH WHICH TO RETALIATE. HIS MIND STREAMS *OUTWARDS*...

...AND FLOWS ACROSS THE GALLERY.

ARE THEY DEAD?

OH, NO. THE ZYGONS NEED THEM VERY MUCH ALIVE...

...THEY COLLECT BEINGS FROM VARIOUS WORLDS, SCAN THEIR *BODY-PRINTS* AND USE A RATHER CRUDE *ENERGY/MASS INTERFACE* TO *RE-CREATE* THEMSELVES IN THEIR CAPTIVES' IMAGES.

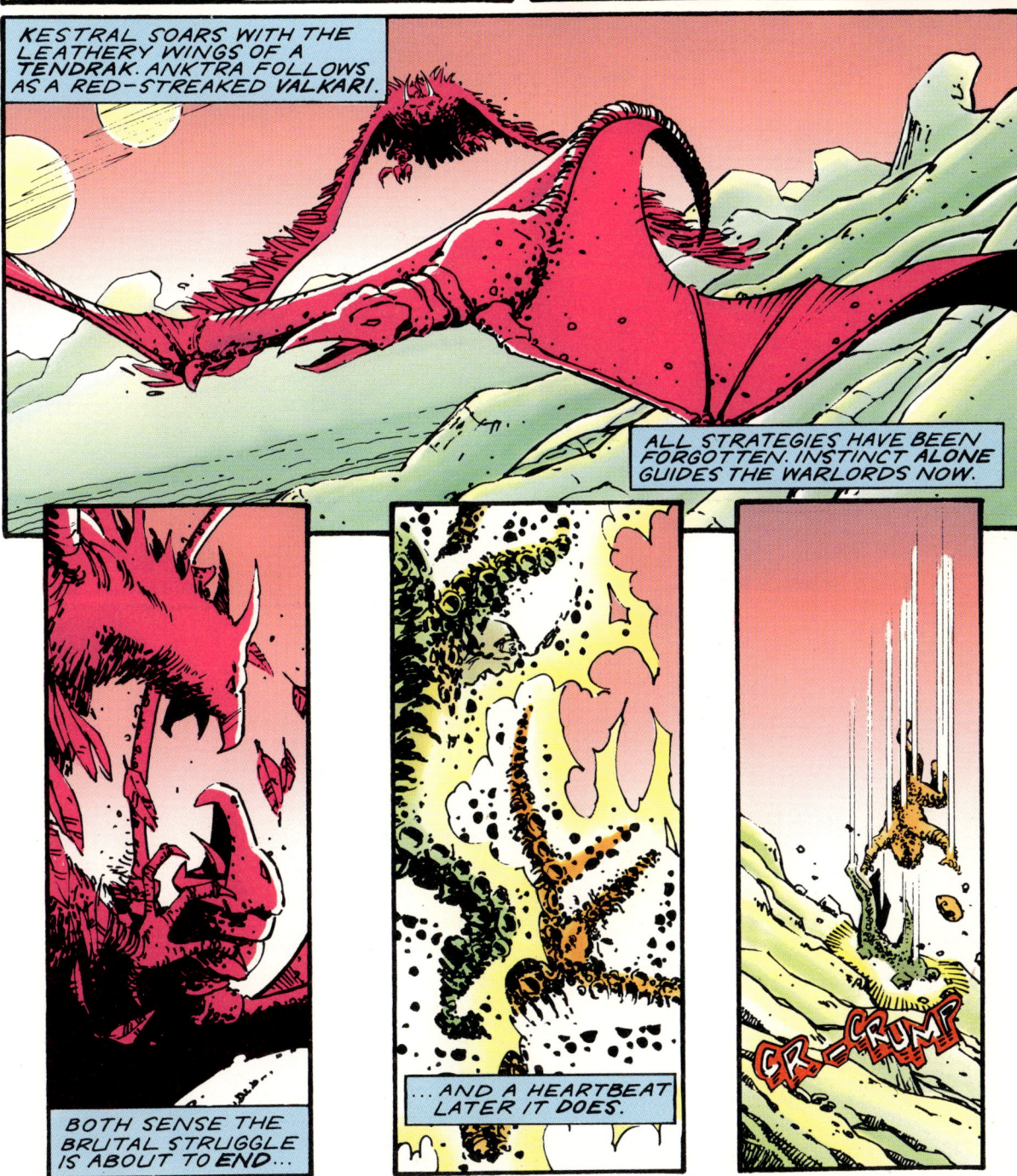

YOU KNOW, I'M SURE THESE PEOPLE HAVE *BETTER* THINGS TO DO THAN STAND AROUND ALL DAY HELPING TWO ZYGONS KILL EACH OTHER

LET'S WAKE THEM UP AND SEE, SHALL WE?

SLUPP
SLUPP

KESTRAL SOARS WITH THE LEATHERY WINGS OF A TENDRAK. ANKTRA FOLLOWS AS A RED-STREAKED VALKARI.

ALL STRATEGIES HAVE BEEN FORGOTTEN. INSTINCT ALONE GUIDES THE WARLORDS NOW.

BOTH SENSE THE BRUTAL STRUGGLE IS ABOUT TO *END*...

...AND A HEARTBEAT LATER IT DOES.

GR-CRUMP

33

WH— WHAT...?

THE BODY-PRINTS... HAVE BEEN WIPED! BUT WHO COULD HAVE—

EXCUSE ME GENTLEMEN; WOULD ONE OF YOU HAPPEN TO BE THE OWNER OF A BLACK DYNACRON-DRIVE STAR-CRUISER?

I'M AFRAID YOUR VEHICLE IS BLOCKING TRAFFIC.

THE FINE COULD BE QUITE SEVERE...

LATER...

SURELY THE CREATURES WILL KILL THE ZYGONS, DOCTOR...?

WELL, IT WAS A DISTINCT POSSIBILITY UNTIL I POINTED OUT THAT NONE OF THEM COULD PILOT A ZYGON SPACECRAFT

THEN THEY ALL DECIDED TO CALM DOWN A LITTLE.

YOU KNOW, I'VE FOUND TODAY VERY RELAXING, LEELA — WE SHOULD TAKE A BREAK MORE OFTEN.

AS YOU SAY, DOCTOR...

34

Andrew Pixley's WHOFAX

Stories counted in their original UK transmission format (e.g. *The Five Doctors* as 1, *Resurrection of the Daleks* and *Attack of the Cybermen* as 2) including *Shada* as six episodes. This gives a total of 156 stories and 701 episodes.

THE DOCTOR	Stories	Episodes
First Doctor [1]	31	135
Second Doctor [2]	25	128
Third Doctor [3]	26	130
Fourth Doctor [4]	45	181
Fifth Doctor [5]	21	70
Sixth Doctor [6]	10	33
Seventh Doctor [7]	12	42

Not including appearances in 'flashbacks' from stock footage (e.g. *Earthshock, Resurrection of the Daleks*, etc.) or the pilot.

[1] From *An Unearthly Child* to *The Power of the Daleks* Episode One, plus *The Three Doctors* and *The Five Doctors* (played by Richard Hurndall). Excluding *The Keys of Marinus: The Screaming Jungle*, *The Keys of Marinus: The Snows of Terror* and *Mission to the Unknown* in which the Doctor does not appear, and also *The Massacre: The Sea Beggar* and *The Massacre: Priest of Death* in which William Hartnell plays the Abbot of Amboise only. Including *The Celestial Toymaker: The Dancing Floor* in which the Doctor's hand is played by Albert Ward, *The Tenth Planet* Episode 3 in which the Doctor is played by Gordon Craig, episodes where the Doctor is only heard (e.g. *The Celestial Toymaker: The Hall of Dolls*) and episodes where Hartnell appears in the reprise only (e.g. *The Dalek Invasion of Earth: The End of Tomorrow*).

[2] From *The Tenth Planet* Episode 4 to *The War Games* Episode Ten, plus *The Three Doctors, The Five Doctors*, and *The Two Doctors*. Including *The Wheel in Space* Episode 2 in which Chris Jeffries plays the Doctor, *The Seeds of Death* Episode Four in which Tommy Laird plays the Doctor, and episodes in which Patrick Troughton appears in the reprise only (e.g. *The Web of Fear* Episode 2).

[3] From *Spearhead from Space* to *Robot* Part One, plus *The Five Doctors*.

[4] From *Planet of the Spiders* Part Six to *Castrovalva* Part One, plus *The Five Doctors*. Including *Shada*.

[5] From *Logopolis* Part Four to *The Caves of Androzani* Part Four.

[6] From *The Caves of Androzani* Part Four to *Time and the Rani* Part One, with Sylvester McCoy as the Doctor in this latter episode.

[7] From *Time and the Rani* Part One to *Survival* Part Three.

THE COMPANIONS AND UNIT TEAM

Susan Foreman [1]	11	52
Ian Chesterton [2]	16	77
Barbara Wright [3]	16	74
Vicki [4]	9	38
Steven Taylor [5]	10	45
Katarina [6]	2	5
Sara Kingdom [7]	1	9
Dorothea (Dodo) Chaplet [8]	6	19
Polly [9]	9	36
Ben Jackson [10]	9	36
Jamie McCrimmon [11]	22	116
Victoria Waterfield [12]	8	42
Brigadier Lethbridge-Stewart [13]	23	103
Zoe Herriot [14]	9	49
Corporal/Sergeant/RSM Benton [15]	16	61
Elizabeth Shaw [16]	5	25
Josephine Grant [17]	15	77
Captain Michael Yates [18]	10	42
Corporal Bell [19]	2	5
Sarah Jane Smith [20]	19	81
Harry Sullivan [21]	7	25
Leela [22]	9	40
K9 Mark I [23]	5	19
K9 Mark II [24]	16	57
Romanadvoratrelundar (A) [25]	6	26
Romanadvoratrelundar (B) [26]	12	47
Adric [27]	13	44
Nyssa [28]	14	48
Tegan Jovanka [29]	20	65
Vislor Turlough [30]	11	32
Kamelion [31]	3	7
Perpugilliam (Peri) Brown [32]	10	33
Melanie Bush [33]	5	20
Dorothy (Ace) [34]	9	31

[1] From *An Unearthly Child* to *The Dalek Invasion of Earth: Flashpoint*, plus *The Five Doctors*.
[2] From *An Unearthly Child* to *The Chase: The Planet of Decision*.

[3] From *An Unearthly Child* to *The Chase: The Planet of Decision*. Excluding *The Sensorites: A Race Against Death, The Sensorites: Kidnap* and *The Web Planet: Escape to Danger*.
[4] From *The Rescue: The Powerful Enemy* to *The Myth Makers: Horse of Destruction*. Excluding *Mission to the Unknown*.
[5] From *The Chase: Planet of Decision* to *The Savages* Episode 4. Excluding *Mission to the Unknown*.
[6] From *The Myth Makers: Horse of Destruction* to *The Daleks' Master Plan: The Traitors*.
[7] From *The Daleks' Master Plan: The Traitors* to *The Daleks' Master Plan: Destruction of Time*.
[8] From *The Massacre: Bell of Doom* to *The War Machines* Episode 2.
[9] From *The War Machines* Episode 1 to *The Faceless Ones* Episode 6. Excluding *The Power of the Daleks* Episode Four and *The Faceless Ones* Episodes 3, 4, and 5.
[10] From *The War Machines* Episode 1 to *The Faceless Ones* Episode 6. Excluding *The Power of the Daleks* Episode Five and *The Faceless Ones* Episodes 3, 4, and 5.
[11] From *The Highlanders* Episode 1 to *The War Games* Episode Ten, plus *The Five Doctors* (as a 'phantom') and *The Two Doctors*. Excluding *The Enemy of the World* Episode 4.
[12] From *The Evil of the Daleks* Episode 2 to *The Wheel in Space* Episode 1. Excluding *The Enemy of the World*.
[13] Comprising *The Web of Fear* Episodes 2 to 6 (played by Maurice Brooks in Episode 2), *The Invasion* Episodes 2 to 8, *Spearhead from Space* to *The Claws of Axos* (excluding *Inferno* Episode 5 where Nicholas Courtney only plays the Brigade Leader), *Colony in Space* Episodes One and Six, *The Dæmons, Day of the Daleks, The Time Monster* Episodes One to Four and Six, *The Three Doctors, The Green Death, The Time Warrior* Part One, *Invasion/Invasion of the Dinosaurs, Planet of the Spiders* Parts One, Two, and Six, *Robot, Terror of the Zygons, Mawdryn Undead, The Five Doctors* and *Battlefield*.
[14] From *The Wheel in Space* Episode 2 to *The War Games* Episode Ten, plus *The Five Doctors* (as a 'phantom'). Excluding *The Invasion* Episode Three.
[15] Comprising *The Invasion* Episodes 1 to 3, 5, 6, and 8, *The Ambassadors of Death* Episodes 5 and 7, *Inferno* Episodes 1, 2, 6, and 7 (John Levene plays the Platoon Under Leader only in Episodes 3 to 5), *Terror of the Autons* Episodes One, Two, and Four, *The Mind of Evil* Episodes Two to Six, *The Claws of Axos, The Dæmons, Day of the Daleks* Episodes One, Two, and Four, *The Time Monster* Episodes One to Four and Six, *The Three Doctors, The Green Death* Episodes Four to Six, *Invasion/Invasion of the Dinosaurs, Planet of the Spiders* Episodes One and Two, *Robot, Terror of the Zygons* and *The Android Invasion* Part Four (Levene plays an android only in Parts Two and Three).
[16] From *Spearhead from Space* to *Inferno*, plus *The Five Doctors* (as a 'phantom'). Excluding *Inferno* Episode 5, in which Caroline John plays the Section Leader only.
[17] From *Terror of the Autons* to *The Green Death*.
[18] Comprising *Terror of the Autons* to *The Claws of Axos, The Dæmons, Day of the Daleks* Episodes One, Two, and Four, *The Time Monster* Episodes One to Four, *The Green Death* Episodes Four to Six, *Invasion of the Dinosaurs, Planet of the Spiders, Robot* and *The Five Doctors* (as a 'phantom').
[19] Comprising *The Mind of Evil* Episodes One to Four and *The Claws of Axos* Episode One.
[20] From *The Time Warrior* to *The Hand of Fear*, plus *The Five Doctors*. Not including *K9 and Company: A Girl's Best Friend*.
[21] From *Robot* to *Terror of the Zygons*, plus *The Android Invasion* Part Four (Ian Marter plays and android only in Parts Two and Three).
[22] From *The Face of Evil* to *The Invasion of Time*.
[23] From *The Invisible Enemy* Part Two to *The Invasion of Time* Part Six. Excluding *Image of the Fendahl* Parts Two and Three.
[24] From *The Ribos Operation* to *Warriors' Gate*, including *Shada* Parts Two to Five. Excluding *The Ribos Operation* Part Two, *The Power of Kroll, Destiny of the Daleks* Parts Two to Four, *City of Death, The Leisure Hive* Parts Two to Four and *State of Decay* Part Two.
[25] From *The Ribos Operation* to *The Armageddon Factor*.
[26] From *Destiny of the Daleks* to *Warriors' Gate*, plus *Shada* and *The Five Doctors*.
[27] From *Full Circle* to *Earthshock*, plus an illusion in *Time-Flight* Part Two and a memory in *The Caves of Androzani* Part Four.
[28] From *The Keeper of Traken* to *Terminus*, plus a memory in *The Caves of Androzani* Part Four. Excluding *Logopolis* Part One and *Kinda* Parts Two and Three.
[29] From *Logopolis* to *Resurrection of the Daleks*, plus a memory in The Caves of Androzani Part Four. Excluding Arc of Infinity Part One.
[30] From *Mawdryn Undead* to *Planet of Fire*, plus a memory in *The Caves of Androzani* Part Four.
[31] Comprising The King's Demons, Planet of Fire and as a memory in The Caves of Androzani Part Four.
[32] From *Planet of Fire* to *The Trial of a Time Lord* Part Eight.
[33] From *The Trial of a Time Lord* Part Nine to *Dragonfire*.
[34] From *Dragonfire* to *Survival*.

RECURRING CHARACTERS

The Monk [1]	2	7
Professor Edward Travers [2]	2	12
The Master (A) [3]	8	37
Omega [4]	2	7
Davros [5]	5	15
The Master (B) [6]	2	8
Borusa [7]	4	13
The White Guardian [8]	3	4
The Black Guardian [9]	4	13
The Master (C) [10]	11	28
The Castellan [11]	2	5

Lytton [12]	2	4
The Rani [13]	2	6
Sabalom Glitz [14]	2	9

[1] *The Time Meddler* and *The Daleks' Master Plan: Volcano* to *The Daleks' Master Plan: Escape Switch.*
[2] *The Abominable Snowmen* and *The Web of Fear.*
[3] *Terror of the Autons, The Mind of Evil* Episodes Two to Six, *The Claws of Axos, Colony in Space* Episodes Four to Six, *The Dæmons, The Sea Devils, The Time Monster, Frontier in Space* Episodes Three to Six.
[4] *The Three Doctors* Episodes Two to Four and *Arc of Infinity.*
[5] *Genesis of the Daleks, Destiny of the Daleks* Episodes Two to Four, *Resurrection of the Daleks, Revelation of the Daleks, Remembrance of the Daleks* Parts Three and Four.
[6] *The Deadly Assassin* and *The Keeper of Traken.*
[7] *The Deadly Assassin* Parts One, Two and Four, *The Invasion of Time* Parts One to Three, Five and Six, *Arc of Infinity* and *The Five Doctors.*
[8] *The Ribos Operation* Part One, a voice in *The Stones of Blood* Part One, *Enlightenment* Parts One and Four.
[9] *The Armageddon Factor* Part Six, *Mawdryn Undead, Terminus, Enlightenment.*
[10] *The Keeper of Traken* Part Four, *Logopolis, Castrovalva, Time-Flight, The King's Demons, The Five Doctors, Planet of Fire* Parts Two to Four, *The Caves of Androzani* Part Four (as a memory), *The Mark of the Rani, The Trial of a Time Lord* Parts Thirteen and Fourteen, *Survival.*
[11] *Arc of Infinity* and *The Five Doctors.*
[12] *Resurrection of the Daleks* and *Attack of the Cybermen.*
[13] *The Mark of the Rani* and *Time and the Rani.*
[14] *The Trial of a Time Lord* Parts One, Two, Three, Four, Thirteen, Fourteen, and *Dragonfire.*

MONSTERS

	Stories	Cameos
The Daleks [1]	16	7
The Cybermen [2]	9	6
The Cybermats [3]	3	–
The Yeti [4]	2	3
The Ice Warriors [5]	4	2
The Autons and Nestenes [6]	2	–
The Silurians [7]	2	–
The Ogrons [8]	2	1
The Sea Devils [9]	2	1
The Sontarans [10]	4	1
The Mara [11]	2	–
Sil and the Mentors [12]	2	–

[1] *The Daleks, The Dalek Invasion of Earth, The Chase, Mission to the Unknown, The Daleks' Master Plan, The Power of the Daleks, The Evil of the Daleks, Day of the Daleks, Frontier in Space, Planet of the Daleks, Death to the Daleks, Genesis of the Daleks, Destiny of the Daleks, Resurrection of the Daleks, Revelation of the Daleks, Remembrance of the Daleks* plus *The Space Museum, The Wheel in Space, The War Games, The Mind of Evil, Logopolis, Mawdryn Undead, The Five Doctors*
[2] *The Tenth Planet, The Moonbase, The Tomb of the Cybermen, The Wheel in Space, The Invasion, Revenge of the Cybermen, Earthshock, Attack of the Cybermen, Silver Nemesis* plus *The War Games, The Mind of Evil, Carnival of Monsters, Logopolis, Mawdryn Undead, The Five Doctors*
[3] *The Tomb of the Cybermen, The Wheel in Space, Revenge of the Cybermen*
[4] *The Abominable Snowmen, The Web of Fear* plus *The War Games, Mawdryn Undead, The Five Doctors*
[5] *The Ice Warriors, The Seeds of Death, The Curse of Peladon, The Monster of Peladon* plus *The War Games, The Mind of Evil*
[6] *Spearhead from Space, Terror of the Autons*
[7] *Doctor Who and the Silurians, Warriors of the Deep*
[8] *Day of the Daleks, Frontier in Space* plus *Carnival of Monsters*
[9] *The Sea Devils, Warriors of the Deep* plus *Frontier in Space*
[10] *The Time Warrior, The Sontaran Experiment, The Invasion of Time, The Two Doctors* plus *Logopolis*
[11] *Kinda, Snakedance*
[12] *Vengeance on Varos, The Trial of a Time Lord:* Episodes 5 – 8

THE Changeling Years

By
Gareth Roberts

Brenda Jones had had more than enough. Fourteen years she'd been married to Harry and never had he so much as lifted a cloth. Their idle son Peter was no better, stuck up in his room with that rotten pop music blaring 'till all hours. And as for young Debbie, gallivanting about with that crowd of lads... It was all *too* much.

Brenda took down her old suitcase from the wardrobe, threw in her few belongings and slammed the lid down. She took a deep breath. Yes, of course she was doing the right thing. If she didn't leave now, she *never* would.

And then the voice whispered: *Think about it, Brenda, love. You know you don't want to leave. Not really. You want to stay here, with your family.*

Brenda had often heard the Voice. It spoke to her whenever she felt depressed or lonely, offering guidance and reassurance. Its suggestions always seemed so sensible and practical.

That's it, Brenda. Have yourself a nice long lie-down and forget all of this silly leaving nonsense.

Brenda smiled and nodded. The Voice was right, as always. She let the suitcase fall from her grip and slipped back onto her bed.

There, that wasn't difficult, was it? said the Voice. *You deserve some time to yourself. And in the morning you'll feel as right as rain.*

Brenda yawned and closed her eyes. She hoped that she would sleep well tonight. Recently, her dreams had been disturbing, with strange guns and big silver helicopters in them. It was a bit like something out of one of those space programmes on the telly. Tonight, she knew somehow, the Voice would help her dream sensible dreams about knitting patterns or party cakes. She mumbled contentedly and fell asleep.

The bedroom door opened and two tall, thin figures walked in. They wore long black robes and their heads were concealed under hoods. The first opened Brenda's suitcase and put everything back where it belonged. The second produced a syringe from the folds of his cloak. He rolled up Brenda's sleeve and applied it to her forearm.

Well done, the Voice told them. *Return to the duty room. I'll call you again if there's a relapse. This specimen has been unreliable of late, although the test results have been fascinating.*

Nearby, a blue light began to flash illogically in mid-air. A few seconds later, the police box shell of the TARDIS faded up noisily from transparency.

The door flew open and the skin-clad Leela sprang out, every sense alert. Her eyes darted from side to side as she took in her surroundings. This place was not as the Doctor had described it.

"Get back inside, quickly!" The Doctor's curly head popped indignantly from the TARDIS. "You can't go around dressed like tat in the middle of..." His voice trailed off as he looked around. "London?"

"I do not like this British Museum, Doctor," said Leela. "Where are the treasures of art and science?"

The Doctor snorted. "This isn't the British Museum." He nodded up at the blazing sun and loosened his scarf. "I don't think it's even the British Isles. I thought I'd fixed that space/time overlap."

The TARDIS had materialised between two large, featureless concrete blocks that dwarfed it. Exactly identical blocks stretched away in each direction. Beyond them, the time travellers glimpsed a high wire security fence.

"I do not like this place, Doctor," repeated Leela. "I sense evil all around us."

"Nonsense," said the Doctor as he strode off nonchalantly. "Why do you *always* have to be so melodramatic?"

Leela trailed after him. There was no sign of life, but she was beginning to regret leaving her knife in the TARDIS, where the Doctor had been using it to peel potatoes. "So, where are we?"

"Well, we're definitely on Earth," he replied. "One of the desert regions, I think, but I can't place the period from these buildings." He stopped to examine the nearest. "Could be some sort of industrial complex." He walked along the length of the wall, searching for a way in. "There must be a door along here."

Leela waited at the corner of the block. She did not share the Doctor's confidence about this strange place.

Suddenly a raucous clattering came from above. Leela looked up and saw two large helicopters glinting in the cloudless blue sky. "Doctor!" she cried. "Beware, flying beasts!"

The Doctor hurried back up to her, shading his eyes to make out the machines.

Leela tugged at his arm. "Quick! The TARDIS!"

He shook her off. "Good. Perhaps now we can find out where we are." As the helicopters hovered closer he stepped into the open and waved up at them. "Hello!"

The Doctor's optimism was answered by a hail of bullets from the helicopters. He flung himself to the ground. As the pilots wheeled about for another attempt, he picked himself up and ran, with Leela,

39

for cover between two blocks, to their right. An alarm began to sound and a voice called out: *Rogue specimen has been sighted by air patrol in Red Sector Five. Repeat, rogue specimen in Red Sector Five.*

The Doctor pulled Leela flat against a wall. It's shadow kept them from sight as a squad of cloaked, hooded figures hurried past. Each carried a long-nosed rifle.

Leela stamped her foot. "I knew I was right."

"Well, some of us appreciate the occasional surprise in our lives," the Doctor replied tartly. "Ah! Thought so."

"What is it?"

"What does it look like?" The Doctor indicated a door in the block directly opposite them. He ran over and started work with his sonic screwdriver.

Leela's ears pricked up as she sensed the proximity of more guards. They would turn the corner at any moment and discover the Doctor. She made her decision in a fraction of a second. Without a word she darted from cover and ran to meet them.

The guards opened fire instantly. She dodged their bullets with practiced ease and led them away from the Doctor, towards another of the blocks. She ran straight into another guard. Leela kicked the rifle rom his hand and sprang, grappling him to the ground. She pulled back the hood of her opponent and gasped in shock at his features. Thick veins pulsed over a scrawny skull, covered only by a thin layer of flesh. The pursuing guards had now caught up and together they subdued her.

"Wait!"

The command came from a tall, distinguished looking man who emerged from a large building nearby. He carried a clipboard and wore a white coat and a long-suffering expression.

"Kill me now," Leela snarled unwisely. "I do not fear death."

The newcomer sighed. "This must be the rogue the air patrol reported. Twentieth century subculture, by the look of the clothing." He consulted his clipboard. "Twentieth century. That's Block Nineteen."

The hooded guards remained still, uncomprehending.

"Block Nineteen, comprendo?" the man shouted. "And hurry her back. Too long in the open and she may overcome the conditioning."

The guard who had fought Leela nodded and gestured to the others. They started to carry her away. She struggled and kicked frantically. "Take your hands off me, dead one!"

The man watched them disappear around the corner. After fourteen years it was perhaps inevitable that some of the specimens would break through their conditioning and escape from their environments. It was irrelevant now, anyway. The tests were almost over.

The door clicked open at last. The Doctor chuckled. "Bah. No challenge at all. Not fit to be called a lock, really. I've seen better secured piggy-banks. Now, as I recall, Alcatraz..."

His shoulders dropped as he noticed Leela's absence. For a moment he considered going after her. But whatever fate might have befallen her, he stood a better chance of doing something about it from inside. He slipped through the door, shutting it behind him.

The air conditioned corridor within proved as uninspiring as the exterior. The only feature was a metallic hatstand that sported several long white coats. "Oh, that is careless," said the Doctor as he took down the nearest. "People really shouldn't leave these things lying about. It's asking for trouble."

He pushed open an inner door, ascended a flight of stairs and entered a large room filled with consoles, monitors and computers. The Doctor identified one of the machines as a neural scanner and another as a Gersataski scan, used for the recording of mental impulses. White-coated technicians with clipboards bustled about their duties. Five large screens were mounted on the facing wall. Each displayed a different section of a primitive wooden dwelling. The centre screen showed a scruffy looking bearded man dressed in rough woollen garments. He appeared confused and was staring into space, as if listening.

Be still now, Wulfren, somebody was saying. The Doctor noted a small, balding man talking into a flexible microphone on his desk. *Sleep now and fret none the more. That's the way.*

The eyes of the man on the screen closed. He swayed and collapsed onto a pile of straw.

Irritated that nobody had noticed him, a state of affairs he was unaccustomed to, the Doctor coughed. The bald man blinked at him in surprise, then smiled and offered his hand. "Of course, forgive me. You're the Observer, from Head Office. We've been expecting you."

The Doctor pumped the offered had vigorously. He'd been hoping someone would say something like that. "Now, Mister..."

"*Doctor,*" the small man corrected. "Doctor Harold Scorfe."

"I'm so sorry, *Doctor* Scorfe," the Doctor said. "Now, we Observers often say that the best way to observe something is to come to it fresh. I'd like you to explain your work here to me as if I knew *nothing* about it."

Scorfe's smile broadened. It was rare, the Doctor could tell, for anyone to take an interest in him. "Well, as you know, sir, my duty is to ensure the smooth running of the tests in this block."

"Oh, really?" the Doctor said seriously. He pointed at the centre screen. "So what exactly is going on in there now?"

Two guards were now visible on the screen. They were attending to the unconscious body of the bearded man.

Scorfe flushed and coughed. "Well, sir," he said nervously, "now that the tests are coming to an end, it is occasionally necessary to restrain a specimen and reinforce his conditioning. They have been in their environments for fourteen years, after all. Even the illusion of freedom our drugs have given them cannot last forever."

The Doctor looked at another of the screens where a woman and two children were chopping wood. He noticed that small grey discs had been attached to their foreheads, presumably to relay their thoughts to the control room that the Doctor and Scorfe were in.

"You see, sir," Scorfe continued, "each Block contains a perfectly recreated historical environment, in this case the first century AD. The psycho-sociological data we discover from each period is collated and stored away by my staff here, ready to be cross-checked with the findings of the other Blocks."

The Doctor gave an official sounding grunt of approval. "You're certain that the conditioning is sound?" he asked. "The specimens *still* believe themselves to be living in the past?"

"Oh yes, sir," Scorfe replied. "Their previous lives have been wiped from their minds. And I firmly believe they are happier here. I mean to say, sir, the inner cities are *so* depressing."

The Doctor nodded. "Yes, ghastly. Well, thank you, Doctor Scorfe. Now, I really must be going." He made for the door.

"Wait a moment," called Scorfe. "What is *that*?"

The Doctor turned. Scorfe was pointing at the trailing ends of his scarf, which dangled from the tails of his disguise. "Ah,' the Doctor said. He beckoned Scorfe over and whispered, "It's a new security device developed by Head Office."

"Really?" boggled the scientist, completely taken in.

The Doctor unbuttoned his white coat, hoisted up his scarf and looped it around Scorfe's legs. "There you see?"

Scorfe stared down, confused. "And then, sir?"

"And then you do this," said the

41

Doctor. He pulled both ends and Scorfe tumbled to the floor. His colleagues turned and looked in amazement.

The Doctor threw off his disguise and collected his scarf. "Sorry to disturb you," he said and rushed off. He threw open the inner door – to be confronted by a squad of guards.

Brenda was setting the table when Harry burst into the room. She hadn't seen him so excited in years.

"Bren, love. You'll never believe *this!*"

"What is it? Can't you see I'm busy?"

"No love, listen. There's a cavewoman in the kitchen!"

Brenda sighed. "Oh change the record, Harry. I've had about all I can..." she trailed off as a young woman dressed in skins walked into the dinning room. "Who the ruddy heck are you?"

"My name is Leela," the girl replied proudly. Her eyes lit up as she examined the table. She reached for the breadknife. "A good weapon, at last."

The Joneses stood in silent amazement as the intruder paced their carpet like a panther. "Why do you not take arms against those who have imprisoned you?" she shouted, angrily.

Brenda heard the Voice again. *Duty guards, return immediately to Block Nineteen. An error has occurred. The rogue you returned is not contemporary and must be removed to prevent cross cultural contact.*

As if on cue, two cloaked figures burst in. The cavewoman moved in a blur, knocking both to the ground in a flurry of punches and high kicks.

She looked up at Brenda and Harry. "*Now* will you fight?"

Brenda looked down at the bodies. The hood of the first had slipped back to reveal an alien face. It was a Prolon – yes, that was it! The State had called them in to deal with the Portland riots of 2217. Other things were coming back to her. She remembered signing the contract. It had seemed like a good deal; three years of medical tests for this company in return for seven million dollars. But that had been fourteen years ago. She'd been tricked. And her name *wasn't* Brenda Jones.

"Yes, girl," she told Leela. "Yes, I'll fight."

"I've a terrible headache," the Doctor groaned as he recovered consciousness. "Where was I last night? More to the point, where am I now?"

He looked up from the chair he was strapped into. Standing over him were two hooded guards and a middle-aged woman, dressed in black.

"This is our control centre, Doctor," said the woman, gesturing around at the chattering machinery surrounding them. "I am the Director of the tests."

The Doctor smiled. "Oh really? How perfectly charming it is, too. All that vacuum forming, very *chic*... By the way, how do you know my name?"

The Director produced a thick roll of computer print-out. "I ran a Gersataski scan on your brain while you were resting, Doctor. It makes fascinating reading. You are obviously quite insane."

"Am I really?" said the Doctor. "I've been wondering about that for centuries. Then again, I suppose it depends on your viewpoint. I'd say it was quite insane to remove people from their homes and drug them into believing they're living in another century. But then, as a lunatic, who am I to judge?"

The Director chuckled. "Before we shoot you," she told him, "I'm going to find out how you got in here and who you work for. But I don't see why I shouldn't indulge your curiosity. I'm rather proud of our work here."

"Oh goody," said the Doctor. "Indulge on." His hands were working frantically on the knots securing them.

"Over the past few centuries," the Director explained, "many alien races have attempted to conquer Earth. All have failed. Nobody knows why."

"Can't imagine," the Doctor mumbled, still tugging at the knots.

"What my company has created here," the Director enthused, "is the greatest sociological study of all time. From our recreation and examination of many different societies, we are about to produce a detailed document on the essential nature of *homo sapiens*. Their strengths and weaknesses. Such information would be of much value to certain... interested parties."

The Doctor's jaw dropped. "You're going to sell out the entire human race?"

The Director nodded. "And retire to the outer planets on the proceeds. But this," she weighed the print-out in her hands, "is almost as exciting. Your mental state is so deluded, Doctor, I've half a mind to publish it."

The Doctor's hands were finally free. "You can't go round publishing people's brains without their permission. That's theft of intellectual property," he spluttered in mock outrage. "I reserve copyright on my insanity!"

The Director waved the guards forward. "Take him away."

"At least let me speak to my agent," the Doctor prattled disarmingly. He then leapt up, knocking the heads of the guards together with ease. He prodded the bodies with the heel of his boot. The hood of one slipped back. "A denizen of Prolix IV, a low-gravity planet in Monocros. Slaves too, eh? How very unethical."

The Director snarled and backed out of the control centre. The Doctor smiled and crossed over to what he guessed was the central console. He flicked a series of switches and the ever-present hum of computer activity ceased instantly. "That should do it," he told himself. "With the power off, there'll be no way to contain the specimens."

Suddenly he heard shots, cries of alarm and a large explosion.

"That was quick," he muttered.

"Doctor?" he heard Leela calling.

"In here," he called back. She ran into the room, knife raised, an expression of joy on her face.

"I have freed the prisoners in Block Nineteen, Doctor," she cried jubilantly. "The rebellion against the dead ones is spreading. We have taken some of their weapons. Come, let us rejoin the struggle."

He shook his head and sighed. "Do you always have to be so enthusiastic?"

"It is good to enjoy war, Doctor," she replied.

"It is much better to enjoy culture," he said firmly. "We're going straight back to the TARDIS and let these people sort things out for themselves."

"They may need our help, Doctor" Leela protested.

"The TARDIS," he said emphatically. "You've done more than enough damage for one day."

Leela sighed and hurried out. Before the Doctor followed her, he picked up the print-out of the mind scan carried out by the Director. He read the first few lines and laughed, heartily.

"Well, I never knew *that*..."

Doctor Who's Infamous Moments in History

Informed by Tim Quinn and Dicky Howett

Since 1963, the DOCTOR has witnessed many timeless moments in history...

"No need to get uppity, CLEO. I just think it would look better on the THAMES EMBANKMENT!"

"POTATOES! TOBACCO! WHATEVER WILL RALEIGH BRING BACK FROM THE NEW WORLD THIS TIME..?"

"YO!"

"PENNY FOR THE GUY?"

The DOCTOR was there at the start of the HUNDRED YEARS WAR...

And at the END!

"TIME'S UP! EVERYONE STOP!"

TOOT

The DOCTOR was a witness to the first STEAM TRAIN.. ..and ADRIC, the first TRAIN SPOTTER!

"WHAT DO YOU MEAN, 'IT'S SLOW'?"

And finally the DOCTOR was there at the birth of JOHN LOGIE BAIRD'S invention..

"YOU ARE WATCHING THE MOST UNIQUE CONTRIBUTION TO SCIENCE SINCE THE DAWN OF MAN. BUT FIRST OVER TO RICHARD AND JUDY FOR THE LATEST HOT FASHION TIPS..!"

WHIRRRRR

Dicky Howett 1993

43

Perfect Day

By Marc Gatiss

It had been, Tegan was forced to admit, quite an adventure; even by the Doctor's standards. And, as he was forever fond of pointing out when there was an unexpected lull in his hectic life, the Doctor's standards were *exacting*. Any man with experience of however many hundreds of years of traumas and vicissitudes certainly earned Tegan's respect, although her opinion of his long-term memory had been taking a few knocks of late. She had been enthralled by his first-hand account of the Battle of Waterloo; how he had stood at Wellington's side as the German mercenaries sealed the fate of the French. She had later been less impressed when told exactly the same story a few days later, although this time the Doctor claimed to have been standing with Napoleon. Perhaps it was possible for him to have been in both places at once. As he approached her, Tegan looked deeply into his impenetrable blue eyes and decided that as far as the Doctor was concerned, you could never be sure about anything.

The double doors of the TARDIS were wide open and a warm breeze wafted into the console room. Outside, a balmy evening was beginning on Kolkokron and Tegan stood watching the Doctor's slow return, her face inclined towards the low range of mountains. Earlier, the Doctor had disappeared in that direction, carting the dormant Gravis in an unlikely wheelbarrow-like contraption, possessed of large, round thruster pads instead of wheels. He had struggled off into the fading pink light with a cherry wave and a strained "Back in a tick", uttered through clenched teeth. Wryly, Tegan wondered whether the thrusters were taking as much of the Tractator's weight as the Doctor had predicted.

"All done and dusted," announced the Doctor happily upon his return. "He's unlikely to get up to much mischief here. I think we've just time for some tea before we collect Turlough and say our farewells to the colonists on Frontios." He went through the doors into the TARDIS, his voice carrying in the still, dusty air. "One for each person and one for the pot. And stir thirty times if you don't have the patience to let it brew..."

Tegan remained sitting on a boulder and didn't even look up as the Doctor's head popped around the doors again. "Tegan? Coming?"

She looked at his eager face and suppressed a smile. His enthusiasm was certainly contagious. But their most recent adventure had set her thinking.

"I was just..." she began and gestured expansively with her hands. The Doctor trotted out of the TARDIS, digging his hands into the pockets of his cricketer's frock-coat and adopting the furrowed brow and jutting lip of a concerned family practitioner. "What's the matter?"

Tegan ruffled her dark hair. "Everything you said. About Earth. About the colonists of Frontios being the last... the last of..."

The Doctor turned away as though he hadn't heard, shielding his eyes and gazing at the sinking pink sun. "Turlough getting you down is he? Something like that? Well, you have to remember, he's an adolescent, Tegan, and liable to be a bit difficult. We were all young once. Even

45

me. And besides, he was an absolute brick on Frontios..."

"Doctor, you're not listening."

"Hmmm?"

"I want to know what happens to my home. In the future. I have a right to know."

"I thought I'd explained," said the Doctor, still not turning round. "The destruction of Earth is a historical fact. Surely you understand that, Tegan? Civilisations rise and fall. Stars grow and die. People, places, galaxies... Nothing is fixed. Otherwise, where would the fun be?"

Tegan got up of the rock and gently caressed her throat, enjoying the warm breeze which nuzzled her skin. "You don't have to treat me with kid-gloves, Doctor," she murmured evenly. "It's just that it never really struck me before. I remember Nyssa telling me about Traken..."

"There you are, then." The Doctor turned on his heels, his hands flapping at his sides. "A case in point." Traken, Nyssa's homeworld, had been destroyed in the flood of entropy released by the Master on Logopolis, around the time that Tegan had first met the Doctor.

Tegan fixed him with a penetrating stare. "But she never saw *exactly* what happened – only from a distance. How it ended. All that history..."

The Doctor crouched down and picked up a handful of crumbly soil, letting it slip through his hands. "The people of Traken were wiped out, Tegan. That's the difference. The colonists on Frontios are living proof of your species' absolute refusal to give in. Earth's time may be up, but humanity itself, with all its foibles, still goes on. Frontios, Refusis, Balanystra..."

"Yes, yes, I know that. And it helps. But I really need to see how it stops. The closing credits..."

"The end of the world?" asked the Doctor quietly. Tegan nodded. "Is that wise?" he continued.

"I'm not a kid..."

"No, no of course not. But we're not talking about a visit to the dentist, Tegan. Watching the destruction of one's homeworld could induce all sorts of nasty traumas. Each of us has an affinity with our own planet. A connection. It runs very deep. Deeper than you can know."

"I *need* to see it," said Tegan, firmly.

The Doctor looked her in the eye and recognised his companion's steely determination. He fiddled with the rather wizened stick of celery in his lapel and said, almost under his breath, "All right. But just a glimpse. We mustn't get *involved*."

If he had expected Tegan's thanks, he was disappointed. She merely nodded, walking with head bowed into the TARDIS. The Doctor gave a last look at the silent landscape. He sniffed resignedly, hoping that the Gravis was indeed out of action, and ducked back inside the Ship. Within a few moments, the hazy air was disturbed by a strangulated, grating whine and the TARDIS disappeared from Kolkokron.

Tegan was standing against the roundeled wall, chewing a thumbnail anxiously. The Doctor shot her a glance and then immediately busied himself at the console, flicking switches and studying screens with an almost feverish intensity. "I just hope this short hop won't queer our pitch," he said quietly.

"Hmmm?"

"Returning to Frontios, I mean. The old girl's taken such a beating of late. I should hate to leave Plantagenet with a sulky Turlough as a farewell present."

The Doctor slipped his spectacles out of his coat and immediately pushed them up onto his forehead, as though forgetting why he had needed them in the first place. He squinted at a fuzzy read-out and then patted his pockets absently in search of an apparently elusive object.

Tegan cleared her throat and pointed to the Doctor's forehead. He myopically peered at her and then, locating the half-frames, popped them onto the bridge of his nose with a cheery smile. "There we are. Nearly there. Just a slight compensation..." He tailed off again and then closed his eyes as the TARDIS materialised with a particularly unsettling bump.

Susha found herself almost laughing. Instinctively, she put a gnarled brown hand to her lips and suppressed the urge but then, shrugging, let herself go, giving voice to a peal of giggles which echoed across the plains. When the fit was over, she wandered to the rain barrel and splashed tepid water into her face. The laughter left a cheerful warmth in her stomach.

Above the broad and dusty land, the sun blazed with unaccustomed ferocity. Susha walked towards the cabin and sat down gratefully in the shade. She glanced at her arthritic wrist where the ancient chronometer she was fond of wearing had left a deep indentation. It didn't matter to her that the twenty-four hour clock had been abandoned a millennia before. It didn't even matter that she had very little cause to know the hour. In fact, as the astronomers had long-since predicted, nothing much mattered any more. Time was almost up.

Susha gently rubbed her wrist, absently wondering where the watch could have got to. It was a great comfort to her. A link to the vanished civilisation. A kinder, better time. And now it was gone. She shrugged.

Cuther hobbled out of the cabin, sunburn showing on the wasted skin of his legs. He shifted the makeshift crutch from one arm to the other and shielded his eyes against the glare.

"Susha?"

The old woman turned, the sun reflecting brilliantly off her round brown eyes. The boy stumbled towards her and she kissed him lightly on the lips. "What'll we do today?" he asked eagerly. Susha shot a quick glance at the sun.

"Do?"

"Yes. It's Penultima Day, isn't it? I counted on the scroll. You said we'd do something on Penultima Day."

So she had. But yesterday had been Penultima Day. She'd thought it better to mislead the boy so that he wouldn't have time to be afraid.

"What would you like to do?"

The boy bit his lip, remembering the fishing he had done at the stream. Or the frenzied music and dancing they had all enjoyed before the colony ships' embarkation.

There was a deep rumble of thunder which Cuther seemed to feel in his bones. He shivered despite the stifling humidity of the day and glanced down at the old woman. He was about to speak when something caught his eye. In the middle distance, shimmered by the heat haze into a rippling azure column, was a tall blue box.

"Central Africa," said the Doctor, closing the TARDIS doors. "In your terms at least. Countries and power blocs have shifted somewhat by now."

Tegan screwed up her eyes against the glare of the sun, feeling immediately uncomfortable in the sticky heat. A wide, flat, yellow plain stretched before them; a few stubby trees struggling through the soil. She had read somewhere that, before the end of the world, there would be one last perfect day. In her imagination, it would have been a balmy, luxurious summer one, the hours sliding gracefully by into a dusky and beautiful final evening. But even as her foot made its first imprint on the parched ground she could feel the sense of of fear in the air, a kind of charged, palpable, electric panic.

The Doctor placed his Panama hat gratefully onto his brow and looked about with a serious disquiet in his eyes. He felt an overwhelming urge to whisper, as though the gravity of the occasion warranted an almost religious reverence. "This is where it all began," he said gently.

Tegan refrained from adding the obvious rejoinder. They both knew that it was all about to end. That was, after all, the reason for their visit.

"I don't know what I expected," she murmured.

"But this isn't it? Oh, Earth has had its great, shining cities, believe me, Tegan. And more empires have risen and fallen since your time than you can count on your fingers and toes. But all the arks will have gone by now. Things are pretty quiet."

Tegan frowned. "There's no-one left? Everyone's gone?"

"Not quite everyone." The Doctor inclined his head towards a heat-shivered figure, struggling painfully across the plain towards them.

Cuther couldn't remember the last time he had seen two such healthy looking individuals. In the months since Reeson and Kane and Luc had departed he had been surrounded by the old and the sick. He stared in wonder at the tall, athletic young man in the funny coat and the fiercely attractive woman by his side. He put all his weight onto the willowy crutch and held up his one good hand. The Doctor reciprocated, searching his erratic memory for a suitable greeting of the time.

"Bless and keep," he offered without much confidence.

"Bless and keep," replied Cuther, grinning. "Who are you?"

The Doctor doffed his hat. "Just visitors."

"Visitors? Weren't you on the arks? There's nothing wrong with you, is there?"

"Not that I know of," said Tegan. "How d'you mean?"

The Doctor touched Tegan lightly on the shoulder and gave an almost imperceptable shake of the head.

"This is where you live, is it?" he cried cheerfully, indicating the distant cabin with his hat.

"Susha and me. That's all. The others... the others that were left I mean, they went a while ago."

"I see. May we...?"

Cuther nodded eagerly and led the way back across the plain to the cabin. "Today is Penultima Day, you know that don't you?"

"Penultima Day?" queried Tegan

"The day before?" suggested the Doctor uncertainly, glancing up at the furiously blazing sun.

"I'm glad you've come. It's good not to be alone. We can do something now. You two, me and Susha." Cuther almost scurried into the cabin, returning a moment later with the old woman. She regarded the Doctor and Tegan with indifferent eyes, grunting as she lowered herself into a chair.

Cuther produced two spindly bottles and held them aloft with glee. "These were for tomorrow. But we have to celebrate... err...?"

"Doctor," said the Doctor. "And Tegan Jovanka."

Cuther smashed the tops off the bottles and poured generous measures of a glutinous mead into four glasses. Susha raised her glass in a stiff hand.

"Health." A cracked smile lit up her face.

Cuther and Tegan toasted in silence.

"Bottoms up," said the Doctor.

There was silence for a while, then Tegan put a gentle hand on Cuther's arm. "Why weren't you on any of the arks?"

The boy laughed without a trace of bitterness and slapped his withered legs. "Isn't it obvious?"

"Only the strongest and fittest could go, Tegan," said the Doctor gravely. "In order for the species to survive."

Tegan's face darkened. "But that's obscene. Is that all we evolve into? A bunch of Nazis?"

"Seems perfectly reasonable to me," muttered Susha, downing her mead in one swift movement. "There was a story my father used to tell me... From one of the old religions..."

"And the animals went in two by two," said the Doctor.

Susha nodded. "Simple reproduction. And my reproductive days are long gone."

The Doctor tilted his hat onto the back of his head and drank the warm liquid thoughtfully. "There's another version of that story."

Susha cocked an eyebrow. "Yes?"

"Yes. Noah took the animals into the ark but he had to leave many, many others behind. The Unicorns, the Centaurs, the Basilisks... Pragmatism is the enemy of diversity."

"Well, I'm content to be a Unicorn," croaked Susha, smiling. "And when tomorrow comes..."

The Doctor looked at her and understanding passed between them.

"Yes, when tomorrow comes, we'll be ready. Won't we, my boy?"

Cuther hobbled across the porch and held Susha tightly.

The Doctor tapped Tegan on the shoulder and rose. "Well, we have to be off."

Cuther detached himself from the old woman. "But I hoped you would stay. We could see it together."

Tegan looked searchingly at the Doctor and smiled. "No. We'll... we'll see it in our own way."

She looked back only once as they crossed the plain towards the TARDIS.

"Well Tegan?" The Doctor's hands were already spread over a console panel.

"How could they be so... *calm* about it?"

The Doctor shook his head. "Perhaps they can feel that it's a natural end. They're at peace with themselves."

He flicked a switch and the scanner screen hummed into life. Tegan could see an astonishing vista of stars and planets, dominated by a livid, boiling sun – a halo of vapours expanding from its disc. She felt the Doctor's arm close around her shoulder and the comforting tones of his voice.

"Brave heart."

And suddenly the sun erupted into molten fire, a dazzling crimson explosion as its mass expanded beyond reason. In the midst of it all, Tegan saw a tiny blue and green planet world vapourise into space. The astonishing fury filled the entire screen until the Doctor shut off the scanner and let his arm fall to his side.

Instead of the grief or rage she had been expecting, Tegan found herself overwhelmed by the sheer beauty of the sight. As the reassuring hum of the console room once again encroached on her senses, she walked over to the Doctor and kissed him on the cheek. "Thank you."

He smiled, a lock of blond hair falling into his eyes. "Yes, well. Let's see what we can do about co-ordinates for the Veruna system, hmmm? All systems go and back to..." His face lit up as he sensed an awful pun. "Back to..."

"Don't say it," said Tegan, a broad grin spreading across her face.

THIRTY YEARS OF DOCTOR WHO IN FICTION

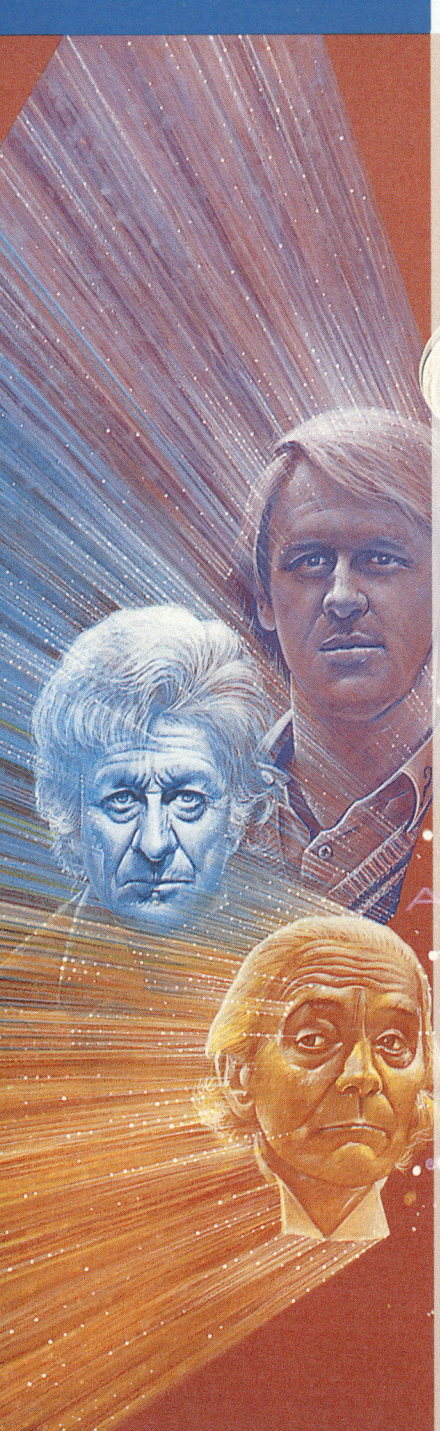

1963 The Doctor and his granddaughter are discovered in the Totter's Lane junk yard by Ian and Barbara
1964 *Susan, the Doctor's granddaughter leaves the TARDIS crew to stay with David Campbell*
1965 The Doctor encounters another of his mysterious race, the Meddling Monk
1966 *The Doctor collapses ill, and his companions Ben and Polly watch in astonishment as he regenerates*
1967 The Doctor travels to the planet Telos and discovers the Cybermen's long-lost tombs
1968 *UNIT, led by Brigadier Lethbridge-Stewart, suffer their baptism of fire against the Cybermen*
1969 The Doctor is captured by his own people, the Time Lords, and put on trial
1970 *The Doctor is exiled to Earth, where he teams up with UNIT to fight alien invaders*
1971 The Doctor's Academy nemesis travels to Earth to try and thwart the Doctor
1972 *The Time Lords bring the first three Doctors together to confront Omega*
1973 The Doctor's freedom to explore time and space is restored. His first visit is to the planet Inter-Minor
1974 *Linx the Sontaran reveals the name of the Doctor's home planet, Gallifrey*
1975 The Doctor returns to Skaro to try and stop the development of the Daleks
1976 *For the first time since his exile, the Doctor visits Gallifrey to combat a disfigured Master*
1977 The Doctor gains a new, robotic, companion – the mobile computer K9
1978 *The Doctor is sent on a mission by the White Guardian to retrieve the legendary Key to Time*
1979 The Black Guardian threatens the Doctor, who fits the Randomiser to the TARDIS to aid his escape
1980 *The TARDIS travels through a CVE and the Doctor is temporarily lost in the pocket universe, E-Space*
1981 The Master usurps a new body and returns to regularly plague the Doctor
1982 *Adric, the Doctor's young companion from E-Space, dies defending Earth from the Cybermen*
1983 Four of the five Doctors combine their skills to defeat the megalomanical Time Lord President, Borusa
1984 *On the planet Sarn the Doctor is forced to destroy his shape-changing robotic companion Kamelion*
1985 For the first time since leaving Totter's Lane, the TARDIS exterior temporarily changes from a Police Box
1986 *On trial once more, the Doctor's prosecutor is revealed to be a possible future incarnation*
1987 The Doctor's companion Mel leaves, despite the fact that the two have never actually met as far as the Doctor can remember
1988 *The Doctor returns to Totter's Lane in 1963, shortly after he left, to fight the Daleks and retrieve the Hand of Omega, a highly destructive Time Lord weapon*
1989 After defeating the Master on the planet of the Cat People, the Doctor and Ace head back to the TARDIS for more adventures...
1990 *The Mandragora Helix re-asserts its influence in twentieth century England*
1991 The Doctor and Ace encounter the malevolent Timewyrm in ancient Mesopotamia
1992 *After Ace angrily abandons the Doctor, he gains a new travelling companion, Bernice Summerfield*
1993 The Third Doctor, the Brigadier and Sarah Jane combine to battle the Paradise of Death

49

The More Things Change

By Andy Lane

My Ma used to tell a story 'bout the day I was born. Always the same, like the details were scratched into her memory the way I used to carve my name in the bark of trees when I was a lad. I never gave it much attention, 'cept for the normal fancies of childhood, but as my life went on, I thought more and more on it. Ma and Pa lived in a pre-fab, out along the banks of the Potomac. They were nicely set up there – Pa done well out of the Dalek invasion. Food was scarce, and he cornered the black market sellin' catfish from the river in Washington and Baltimore. Two ex-Presidents fought over his last fish one day, he said, tearin' each others' hair out and cussin' like good ol' boys. Pa just stood and cheered them on. He never had much time for politics. It was a bad time for most people, what with the diseases an' those little tinpot critters, an' all, but we was okay, for the main.

The marshlands of the Potomac had always been a fever zone, ever since the days of the Foundling Fathers. The stuff the Daleks used was no worse. They never bothered us, either. If they weren't press-gangin' ordinary folks into their minin' teams they was huntin' down rebels in the Blue Ridge Mountains.

And we had food: plenty of it, 'cept we got pretty sick of catfish after a while. But I'm gettin' in advance of myself.

I was tellin' you about the day I was born. That was a few good years before the Daleks came. Ma thought I wasn't due for another week or more, but then her waters broke whilst she was repairin' the satcom unit.

Pa was out with his ultrasonic stunners collectin' the fish. He'd taken the flitter with him, so she couldn't get to the Baltimore Medcentre, and with the satcom out of commission she couldn't call a medic out, even if they'd been able to afford one. So she's lyin' there, she tells us, with the contractions bendin' her double, and prayin' to God that someone would pop by and find her.

She used to act the whole story out, when she told it to us, clutchin' at her stomach, and groanin', and carryin' on like she had a bad case of the gripes. I tried to imagine myself all curled up in there, waitin' to come out, but I couldn't. Anyway, there she was, a-hollerin' and a-screamin', and suddenly there's a cool hand on her brow and a calm voice sayin', "Trust me, I'm the Doctor." She looks up, and there's this man bendin' over her. For a moment she thinks she's died and gone to heaven, because he's got these blond curls and these bright blue eyes, and an aloof expression like he's an Angel descended to Earth, just for her. Then she sees how chubby he is, and the rag-bag clothes he's wearin', and she thinks he must be a traveller of some kind. He's got a gal with him, a nice American gal, and she goes and boils some water for him while he reassures my Ma. Somehow, Ma trusts him, although she normally wouldn't give the time of day to a traveller. Good thing too, because I wouldn't be here otherwise. Ma said that the birth took three hours of strain and pain, and all the time the Doctor was there, reassurin' her and urgin' her on.

'Parently Ma had a difficult time with me – I was twisted in the womb, or somethin', and the Doctor massaged me around in her stomach until I was ready to pop out. All the time, through Ma's tears and screams, the gal was holdin' her hand and castin' anxious glances at the Doctor.

When Pa came back from his fishin' he found Ma asleep and me lyin' in her arms. There was no sign of any Doctor, and no bill either. For a long time he thought she'd been imaginin' it, but I was there as proof.

I had a good childhood. Ma and Pa were strict, but only when I deserved it. I got all my schoolin' from the satellite channels, and I had forests to play in and the river to swim in. There was families nearby, and I had my friends. Yeah, I've got no complaints. And all the time, in the back of my mind, there was this romantic figure called the Doctor who'd appeared at the moment of my birth. I would sit in the forests that led down to the Potomac, watchin' the raccoons foragin' in the undergrowth, and imagine that I wasn't born of Ma and Pa at all, but brought by the stranger and left there. All kids have these fancies.

Arlow, who lived along the river to us and whose Pa ran the local data-collection station for Moonbase weather control, told me once that he was the son of an Egyptian Prince who'd been abducted at birth and left in the wilds of America in the care of a sympathetic but childless couple. I told him he'd seen it on a screen somewhere, but he just struck out at me and we started rollin' around and fightin' in the way that kids do. All my friends were the same: they wanted some romance in their lives, and they weren't adverse to creatin' it.

I was different. I knew there was somethin' 'bout my circumstances that was different from the main. Years passed. The world went to hell and gone. The Dalek things invaded, but the worst we got out of that was the satellite channels goin' down, all but for a handful of rebel transmitters in the mountains bouncin' their signals off the Moonbase antennas. Pa did well out of the Daleks, like I said, and did even better out of their leavin'.

A lot of people wanted dead Daleks or bits of their equipment for souvenirs and for experimentation, but Pa had taken, bought or just plain stolen most of the better stuff. Had the Pentagon, the Butler Corporation, the Smithsonian, IMC, IBM and all the rest sniffin' around, and payin' through the nose for what he had stacked out in his prefab storerooms. Life was very comfortable after that. Very comfortable.

The satellites came back on line, and we were amazed at how the world had changed. Whole countries had been devastated. Coastlines looked different.

More amazin' still was how quickly the world pulled itself back together again. Pa used to sit in the bar with his cronies and boast about how he'd set the world to rights by stockpilin' the Daleks' secrets. It was then that I saw the Doctor again. I say "again", although the first time, of course, I had been too young to pay any attention.

I was in the forest. The Potomac was a glitterin' ribbon, far below me through the oaks. The hum of insects was everywhere: the wet heat sat heavily upon me and caused sweat to prickle my forehead and the small of my back. I was fifteen, and thinkin' about how much I hated the place. I was considerin' signin' on to the Peaceforcers, and seein' somethin' of the world that way. I'd talked to Arlow 'bout it, an' he was fair jumpin' to join up with me. Down below, on the slope that led down to the river, I saw a flash of yellow. Lookin' closer, I noticed a figure pickin' his way through the maze of tree roots. He was wearin' a coat of many colours, and a pair of trousers like nothin' I'd ever seen. His hair was curly, he wasn't fat but he wasn't far short, and I knew straight away who he was. He was the Doctor, and he didn't look a day older than the description that my Ma had given.

I left my place and crept closer, finally hidin' myself in a small clump of rhododendrons. He was bendin' down now, and examinin' the ground. He hadn't seen me, and I didn't want him to. This was a magical moment. He'd come back to take me away. He'd really come back.

"I wandered, lonely as a cloud," he said suddenly, "that floats on high o'er vales and hills, when all at once I saw a crowd, a host, of golden daffodils."

"No daffodils here, Doc," a voice said behind me. I turned, thankful that I was hidden by the bushes, to see a gal walkin' down the slope toward him holdin' a bag. She was so beautiful, it took my breath fair away. I'd seen nothin' like her in the locality – most of the gals I knew were made up to the nines and about as dim as they come – but she was like those classy, unapproachable women they had on the late night satellite shows.

I was in love.

"Oh Peri," the Doctor sighed, "sometimes I despair of you. Where is the poetry in your soul? Where is that rare ethereal beauty of which Will Shakespeare wrote: 'Not marble, nor the gilded monuments of princes, shall outlive this powerful rime; but you shall shine more bright in these contents, than unswept stone, besmear'd with sluttish time.'?"

"I don't have any 'rare, ethereal beauty'" she replied. "I'm from Boston."

The Doctor sighed, and looked around. "Well, have you got what I came for?" he asked petulantly.

"I think so." She didn't seem sure. "If you told me why, it might help. You tell me you want a botanist's opinion, then you use me as a midwife. What's going on?"

"That was unplanned," he admitted. "I thought the forest would be deserted. We couldn't leave the poor woman to die, though, could we? But back to business, we're here to collect plants. What have you found?"

She upended the bag, tipped whole load of plants out on the ground and started to reel off a whole string of foreign-soundin' names. Now, I'm not much of a scholar, but I could see she knew her stuff. I could tell the Doctor was impressed, too, 'cause he started to make comments like a schoolmarm makes to an uppity kid. Well, pretty soon she was gettin' riled, and then pretty soon they was arguin', an' I was sittin' there watchin' my dreams dyin' around me.

I guess it was my own fault. I'd built the Doctor up into this romantic figure, like somethin' out of a Greek myth. Y'know, he appears out of nowhere, helps in my birth, an' then disappears, then reappears fifteen years later. I thought he'd come back for me. I thought he was goin' to take me away to wild an' far places. No such luck: all he is is a spoiled kid who was there collecting Goddamn plants, of all things. Well, I felt like yellin' down to him that he should pull himself together, but he an' the gal had just about come to a Mexican stand-off with the argument.

"Where to next?" she asked. "Back here again, only some other time? I'm getting pretty sick of this place. I mean, America's all very well, and I know it's my home, and I'm grateful that we've come back to visit, but watching the changes, like this, year after year, it's like that story about the man with the painting in his attic that gets older and more decayed while he stays the same age."

"*The Picture of Dorian Grey* by Oscar Wilde, the Doctor announced grandly, lookin' far off into the distance. "A marvellous character, Oscar. You'd have liked him." He glanced over at the gal. "Or perhaps you wouldn't. 'I have nothing to declare but my genius!' Hah! I should have that inscribed above my tomb!"

"They couldn't build one big enough for your ego, she muttered, chuckin' the plants back in her bag. "Come on then, Doc, let's get this over with."

They walked off through the trees, down towards the river. I tried to follow, but my coat caught in the bush, and by the time I'd freed myself, they had gone. I heard a noise like some piece of heavy machinery: I guess it was a flitter of some kind, 'cause the only trace of them I found was the imprint of some kind of landin' gear in the mosses and ferns. As you can guess, I felt as sick as a hog in a pound. I felt like I'd had my chance handed to me on a plate, and it had been snatched away while I wondered whether I was hungry or not.

Anyhow, come my sixteenth birthday, Arlow and I joined the Peaceforcers. They gave us trainin', and education, and big guns, and the chance to make the world safe for, well, for people like us, I guess. I saw action in more corners of the world than I knew existed, over the next twenty years. After the Daleks were thrown out, it was like all bets were off. Superpowers suddenly weren't so super, and the countries we used to call Third World nations had realised that the league table had vanished, and they all had a crack at the title. Little brush-wars started up everywhere: little men with big ideas and a few Dalek guns tried to hold their neighbours to ransom. Our job was to go in and sort it all out.

We were trained in diplomacy, and negotiation, and them good things, but more often than not it all came down to a firefight. Arlow got hisself killed in a stupid quarrel in the red light district of Macau. I held him while he bled to death, talkin' all the time about when we was kids. I cried, but only on the inside. I was a Peaceforcer.

Ma and Pa sent me vids from home, and every couple of years I used to visit them. Things were changin', though. Pa was ill – long term radiation poisonin' from a Dalek weapon he'd picked up and sold on – and Ma wasn't gettin' any younger. The old homestead was goin' to hell as well. Population was boomin', the wheels of industry were turnin', the interim World Government (US Division) had snapped up a whole lot of land for redevelopment, and the river bank looked set to turn into a whole new cityscape. I was given compassionate leave from the Anglo-French war to attend my Pa's recyclin'. I couldn't believe my eyes as the flitter banked low over Virginia and followed the line of the Potomac to home. The forest had gone. From the banks of the brown, sludgy, river, a mass of dirty grey tower blocks had sprung like diseased trees. I couldn't count them, there were so many. Ma lived in Apartment Three Three Five of Floor Fifty Nine of Block

Two Three Three One. After three hours of listenin' to her friends gossip, I had to go for a walk. Was this what I had fought for?

My footsteps echoed across the sterile courtyards and between the vast cliff-faces of the tower blocks. All around me, metalled panels covered the forest floor which I had wandered across so freely as a kid. I felt a strange deadness spread through my chest, as if my childhood was witherin' and dyin' within me. I dropped to my knees, scrabblin' at the seams of the metal plates, but they were too thick, too heavy and too well bevelled together. I could not move them. I stood, wincin' at the pain in my fingertips, and suddenly heard a voice. A theatrical, affectedly British voice.

A familiar voice.

"Well, that should do the trick."

"I still don't see what you're doing."

"My dear pathetic Peri! I fail to see how our little project can possibly puzzle you." They were just around the corner of the nearest block. Quietly, I walked to the edge and peered around. It was him, as I had known it would be, lookin' no older than the last time I had seen him, fifteen years before. The gal was with him, still holdin' the bag.

That part of me which had withered suddenly blossomed again: I felt just like a kid. I even found myself crouchin' down, rememberin' the rough kiss of the rhododendrons and the spring of the ferns beneath my knees.

The Doctor was bendin' over one of the cracks between the metal plates. "Give me another one," he said distractedly, holdin' a hand out towards the gal. She reached into the bag and pulled out a plant, then seemed to pull a part of it off and hand it carefully to him. He carefully pushed the object, whatever it was, down into the crack, then reached into his pocket and sprinkled some glitterin' substance down after it. "That should do it," he said, standin' and rubbin' his hands together in self-satisfaction. "The local populace will be getting quite a surprise in a year or five."

"You're just an old romantic at heart," the gal said. Her smile was like sunshine breaking hesitantly through the clouds after a rainstorm. "Doing all this for people you've never met."

"An old romantic?" He sounded shocked. "Peri, I am *the* romantic!"

"But why? I mean, what's the point in bringing all these flowers forward from the past – their past, I mean – into the future?"

He sighed. "Because they've lost so much, Peri. Millions of square miles of forests, thousands of miles of streams and rivers. Partly, it was the Daleks; but mostly it's them. I want to give them a taste, just a taste, of what they've thrown away."

"It won't make a difference, you know?"

"It will to me." He shook himself. "Come, we have promises to keep, and miles to go before we sleep!"

"What?"

"There's another courtyard through that opening, my dear. Onward the motley." He led the way.

I watched them 'till they were out of sight, vanishin' like a memory. The wind whistled through the man-made canyons. I wanted to follow them, but I was scared that, if I did, they wouldn't be there.

Ma died ten years later, while I was helpin' suppress an' insurrection on the Moon. She threw herself out of the window of Apartment Three Three Five of Floor Fifty Nine of Block Two Three Three One. I didn't make it to the recyclin', but I went back a few months later to clear out her Apartment and make arrangements to sell it. I looked around, trying to remember her, and Pa, but all I could hear was her voice telling me about the strange man who helped with my birth.

I crossed to the window, and looked out at view, the last thing she must have seen. The river was gone, replaced by more apartment blocks.

I let my gaze roam over them. For a moment I thought my eyes were deceivin' me, 'cause there seemed to be a slight fuzz of green in the courtyard, far far below. I went down to check. I felt I already knew, but I had to be sure. Plants were growin' up through the cracks in the metal panels. I recognised them from my childhood – cattails, arrowarum, pickerelweed and thin willow saplings. I bent and sniffed deeply at these magical reminders, these survivors of other, happier times. The scent took me back, and for the first time I cried for my Ma, and my Pa, and myself.

A malfunctioning weapon 'bot took most of my torso away, a few years later, and I was pensioned out of Peaceforce. I never sold Ma's apartment, and I'm glad. I live there now, with machines to keep me alive, and nothin' to do look out onto where the Potomac used to flow and watch the little forest growing at the base of the metal towers, and the ivy climbing up their sides.

I hope I live to see it hit Level Fifty Nine.

But I *know* I'll live to see the Doctor once more before I die.

54

THIRTY YEARS OF DOCTOR WHO IN FACT

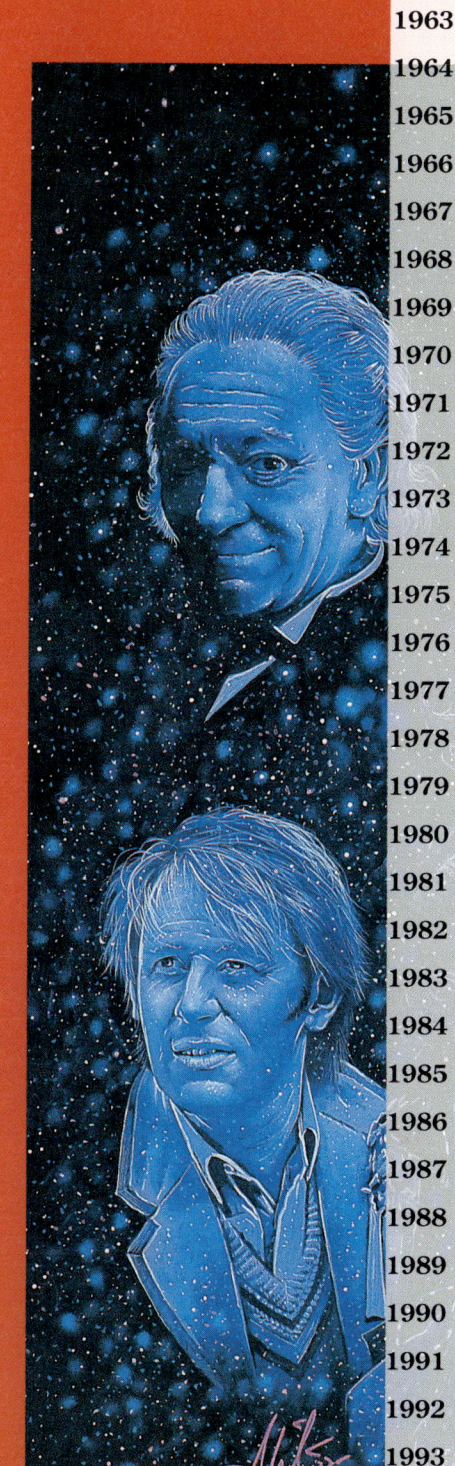

DOCTOR WHO 30th ANNIVERSARY 1963-93

1963   *The world's longest-running science-fiction series begins on 23rd November*

1964   The first location filming for the series is undertaken for Season One's **The Reign of Terror**

1965   *A specially shot trailer for The Web Planet, the first of its kind for the series, is screened*

1966   In the first change of lead actor for the show, Patrick Troughton replaces William Hartnell as Doctor Who

1967   *The Macra Terror features the Doctor's face as part of the series' opening title sequence for the first time*

1968   **The Dominators** is the first story written under a pseudonym. Mervyn Haisman and Henry Lincoln become Norman Ashby

1969   *The first colour filming for the series is undertaken for Spearhead from Space, Jon Pertwee's opening adventure*

1970   Colour Seperation Overlay, a special effects mainstay of the series, makes its debut on **Doctor Who and the Silurians**

1971   *The Dæmons, screened over the Christmas period, becomes the first Doctor Who compilation repeat*

1972   On the wishes of producer Barry Letts, the first radical reworking of the theme music is shelved

1973   *The first Target novelisation of a Doctor Who story is published – a reprint of Doctor Who in an Exciting Adventure with the Daleks*

1974   Tom Baker's opening story, **Robot**, features Outside Broadcast video material for the first time. It later replaces film entirely

1975   *In April, the original Doctor Who, William Hartnell, dies. He often confessed the series had been hard work. "But I loved every minute."*

1976   **Exploration Earth – The Time Machine**, starring Tom Baker and Elisabeth Sladen, is the first **Doctor Who** radio drama

1977   *Doctor Who studio work is undertaken outside BBC London studios for the first time. The Horror of Fang Rock is shot in Birmingham*

1978   **The Stones of Blood**, the one hundredth **Doctor Who** story is transmitted. A celebratory scene is cut from the final script

1979   *The first regular magazine devoted to the programme is published. Doctor Who Weekly makes its first appearance in October*

1980   The Radiophonic Workshop take over the composition of incidental music. A new version of the theme music is implemented

1981   *K9 & Company – the first spin-off from Doctor Who – is screened. It also stars Elisabeth Sladen as Sarah Jane Smith*

1982   Concorde, featured extensively in **Time-Flight**, becomes the most expensive prop seen in the series

1983   *In the Twentieth Anniversary year, fans vote for Revenge of the Cybermen to become the first Doctor Who home video*

1984   **Resurrection of the Daleks** comprises forty-five minute episodes – the first story ever to do so

1985   *The break between Seasons Twenty-Two and Twenty-Three is the longest in the show's history*

1986   The longest **Doctor Who** story, **The Trial of a Time Lord**, is transmitted. It spans fourteen episodes

1987   *Patrick Troughton dies suddenly in America. The Doctor remained "one of the most enjoyable rôles I have ever played."*

1988   A behind-the-scenes documentary is recorded, covering the making of the Twenty-Fifth Anniversary story, **Silver Nemesis**

1989   *Survival is the last new television adventure transmitted by the BBC to date*

1990   The satellite television station BSB devotes a whole weekend to a retrospective of classic **Doctor Who**

1991   *Six minutes of previously unscreened footage is integrated into the home video of The Curse of Fenric – the first release of its kind*

1992   A reconstructed version of **Shada**, the only unfinished **Doctor Who** story, is made available to the public as a BBC Video

1993   Doctor Who celebrates its Thirtieth Anniversary

55

Pulling Strings

By Nigel Robinson

Mel shuddered as the double doors of the TARDIS sighed open and a bitter east wind swept through the control chamber. She glanced over reproachfully at the Doctor who was already shuffling himself into his oversized duffel coat; there were times, Mel decided, when she definitely preferred his earlier persona.

At least that Doctor, the one with the atrocious dress-sense and the wayward waistline, had a taste for the comfortable, good things of life. All this dour-faced one seemed to do was to take her from one urban blight to another storm-swept deathworld; hardly the wonders and delights he'd promised when he'd first snatched her from her comfortable but excruciatingly boring existence in Pease Pottage.

He grinned at her with that infuriatingly superior expression of his, and offered her the fur coat which was hanging from the hat-stand in the corner of the chamber, and whose lurid psychedelic colours hurt her eyes.

The Doctor looked crestfallen as Mel grimaced. "Early Seventies," he remarked, as he helped her into it. "Belonged to a friend of mine. The Seventies will be making a come-back one day, you know – Abba, flares, platform soles . . ."

Mel shrugged in horror and disbelief and wrapped the coat tightly around her, as the Doctor led the way out of the TARDIS.

"So where are we?" she asked as she sheltered under the Doctor's umbrella from the torrential rain, which had already turned the ground into a vicious quagmire. The TARDIS had materialised on a wild open moor in the middle of a storm. Thunder rumbled ominously in the night sky, and sheets of lightning tinged the darkening clouds a cold, metallic blue.

The Doctor smiled and breathed in the fresh, ozone-laden air. "Earth," he said.

"I know that!" said Mel. "There's nowhere else in the universe where the weather can be this bad! But where on Earth?"

"Harrow Green," the Doctor volunteered. "The most haunted village in all England."

Mel frowned. *Harrow Green.* The name rang a distant bell. Suddenly she remembered. "We're near Pease Pottage!" she exclaimed, shouting above the noise of the thunder. "You've brought me home!"

"Well, not quite," said the Doctor, and brought out an elaborate pocket watch from his waistcoat. "It's the early twenty-first century, and Pease Pottage hasn't been your home for at least thirty years . . ."

"What d'you mean? I moved up to London?"

The Doctor tapped his nose. "You went travelling . . ."

"So what are we doing here?" Mel asked.

"I'm a Doctor," her companion said mysteriously. "I'm here to perform a bypass operation."

Mel shook her head and laughed; if the Doctor was going to be enigmatic she certainly wasn't going to give him the satisfaction of knowing that she hadn't the faintest idea what he was talking about.

"You know, Doctor, sometimes I just don't understand you at all."

"Sometimes neither do I," admitted the Doctor. "But to everything there is a reason," he misquoted.

"Bob Dylan?"

"No. John Smith and the Common Men," the Doctor said and pointed in the direction of a small group of buildings just visible on the horizon. "That's where we're needed."

Through the rain Mel could make out the electrified fence which surrounded the compound and the watchtowers manned by armed guards. Surely the Doctor didn't believe they could breach that sort of security?

The Doctor indicated that she should look in the pockets of her psychedelic fur coat. She pulled out two official-looking passes, one of which bore a photograph of the Doctor – the Doctor she was with now – and the other of a terminally hip young woman from the early Seventies.

"So who's Josephine Grant?" she asked, and looked at the insignia on the cover of each of the passes. "And what's UNIT?"

The Doctor grinned and led the way through the mud to the military establishment.

The weasel-faced middle-aged scientist looked up angrily, as the uniformed guards escorted the Doctor and Mel into the laboratory.

"What the hell are these two doing here?" he barked as he took in the sight of the bedraggled Doctor and Mel. "We are at a crucial point in our work. It is essential that I am not disturbed!"

Mel shivered: there was something

57

oddly disconcerting about the scientist as if she had met him somewhere before, a long, long time ago. Things like that irritated her intensely: she was supposed to have a photographic memory after all. So why couldn't she remember where she'd seen Professor Clubman – as his name-tag identified him – before?

The Doctor shrugged off the attention of the two UNIT guards and strode up to Clubman, hand outstretched in greeting.

"Professor Lionel Clubman, I presume?" he said, and introduced himself as Doctor John Smith. Before the nonplussed scientist could reply the Doctor turned to the man's two white-coated colleagues. "And these are...?"

"My name is Professor Christine Roupie," said an attractive Frenchwoman in her thirties, and indicated the long-haired untidily-dressed man by her side. "And this is Doctor Berndt Lehmann..."

"An international team, I see," remarked the Doctor. "And your specialities are?"

"I'm an archaeologist, and a physicist," Roupie replied. "Berndt here is a biologist and anthropologist..."

"Look, just what are you doing here?" demanded Clubman. "This is a top-secret research establishment."

"And I'm a top-secret advisor," said the Doctor peevishly.

"That's right, sir," said one of the guards. "He did have a UNIT pass..."

The Doctor saw that the scientists were still none-too-impressed by this so to divert their attention away from further questioning he took an animated interest in the banks of machinery lining the wall, and the plate-glass window which looked into an empty chamber. He clapped his hands with glee and strode over to the instruments.

"I say! Is this really what I think it is?" he asked eagerly, like a little child opening his presents on Christmas morning.

Clubman glowered at him. "You seem remarkably well-informed, Doctor 'Smith'. *You* tell me."

"It's a tachyon accelerator, isn't it?" the Doctor said. From the astonished looks on the faces of Clubman, Christine and Lehmann it was plain that he had guessed correctly.

"What's a tachyon accelerator?" asked Mel.

"A rudimentary time-machine," the Doctor explained, and turned back to Clubman. "You're experimenting with time technology, aren't you?"

Clubman remained silent, but Christine and Lehmann exchanged a look of amazement at the Doctor's knowledge.

"And where else to experiment than at Harrow Green, the most haunted place in all England?" the Doctor continued. "There have always been stories of ghosts and timeslips in this area. Harrow Green stands on the temporal-spacial nexus, where the strands of time are the weakest and easiest to break through..."

"How could you know that?" asked Christine. "We are only now making studies in that area..."

"Top secret," teased the Doctor, and then added: "It'll never work, you know..."

"All our researches say it will," insisted Lehmann. "We have already sent animals back in time..."

"Animals?" asked the Doctor. "Surely you weren't thinking of sending a human being back in time with this contraption, were you?"

Clubman refused to answer, but Christine stepped forward. "As a matter of fact, yes," she said. "Berndt here has volunteered... he will be the first person to travel backwards in time..."

The Doctor affected an expression of great concern. "But he can't - you mustn't..." he said – rather *too* melodramatically, thought Mel.

"And who are you to say we shouldn't?" barked Clubman.

"I'm the Doctor!" insisted the Doctor, as if that explained everything. "If you've done your researches properly you'd have discovered that human tissue can't withstand tachyon bombardment – "

"Our tests have shown us that animals can – " began Doctor Lehmann.

"Animals! Guinea Pigs! Hamsters!" spluttered the Doctor with contempt. "Have you brought any of them back?"

"Well, no..." Christine admitted.

"And if you did, you'd find their bodies destroyed, their brains burned out..." The Doctor looked knowingly at Clubman. "Time travel is not meant for mammals – well, except certain time sensitives

58

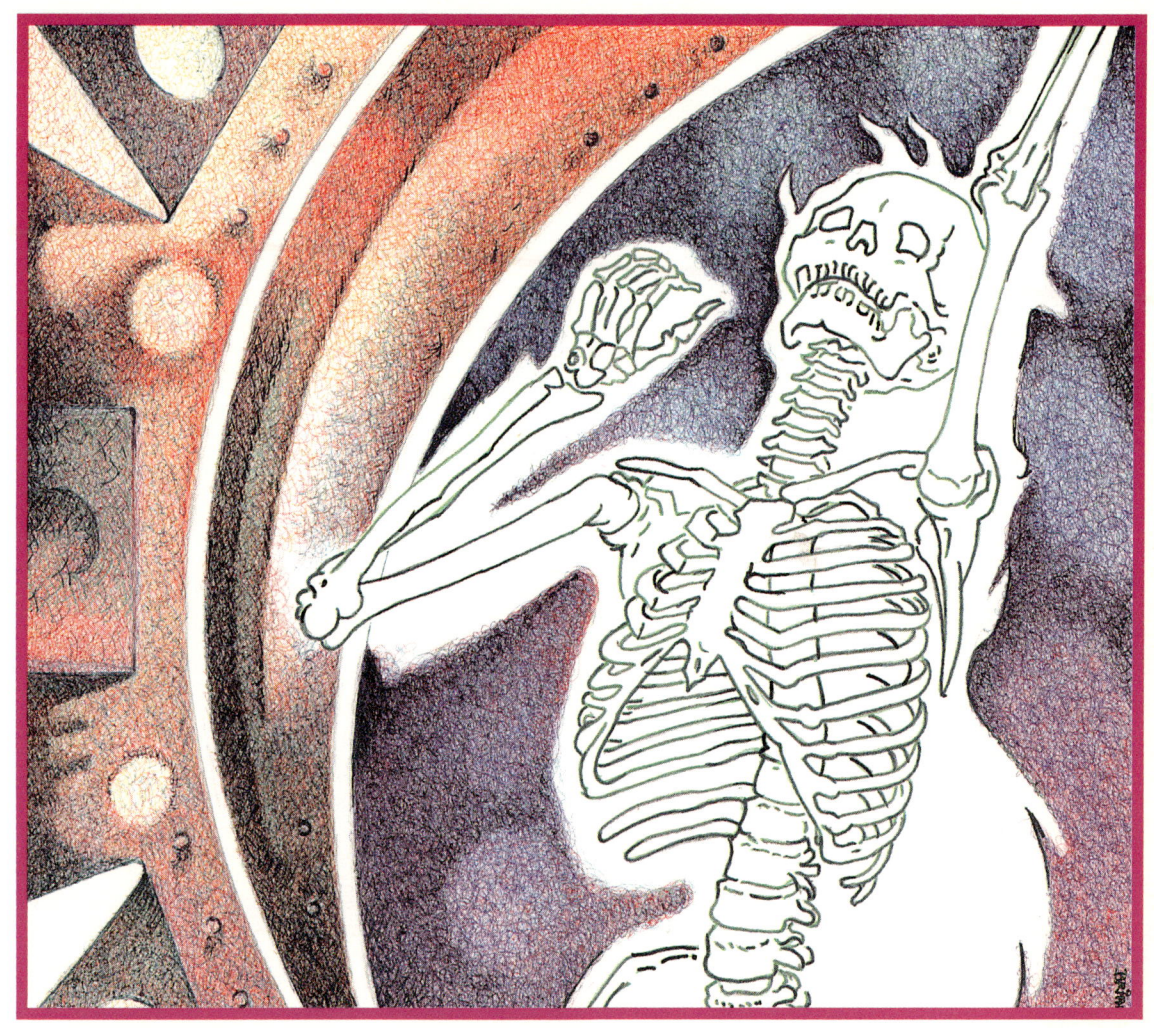

– and especially not for human beings . . ." he insisted. "Better to live in the present than to relive the past . . . "

"Perhaps you would explain your theory?" asked Christine, who of the three scientists seemed the most reasonable.

"I'd be delighted to!" the Doctor said and seated himself down at a desk, casually throwing a whole pile of papers from the desk onto the floor at the same time.

After twenty minutes of what, to Mel, sounded like some top-rate gobbledegook Christine looked over at Clubman. There was a worried look on her face.

"Lionel, if we could perhaps have a meeting?"

Clubman harrumphed angrily, but nevertheless followed Christine and Lehmann out of the room.

"So what was all that about?" asked Mel when the three scientists had gone.

"Top-rate gobbledegook," the Doctor confirmed brightly, "with not a word of truth in it."

"So they're right then? This tachyon accelerator will be able to send people back in time?" she asked.

"Once only," agreed the Doctor. "The strain of breaking through the time lines should should produce a nice little explosion."

"Shouldn't you have told them that then?"

"No need – they'll have plenty of warning and time to get out . . . " he said knowingly. "But with the machine destroyed whatever – or whoever – uses it will never be able to get back to the present day."

Mel looked accusingly at the Doctor: he was definitely up to something. "Are you meddling again, Doctor?"

"I never meddle, Mel," he replied, without the slightest conviction.

The three scientists were arguing with Christine looking sadly at Clubman. "I'm sorry, Lionel," she said, and meant it. "Until we re-examine the Doctor's theories there must be a halt to the time-travel experiments . . . "

"But we are at breakthrough point!" he barked. "We can't halt the experiment now, just because some little man wanders in here and says we can't . . . "

"He's not just 'some little man', he's UNIT's Scientific Advisor, and from all accounts a trusted friend of Brigadiers Lethbridge-Stewart and Bambera," Christine pointed out. "Lionel, you're outvoted, I'm afraid. And we simply cannot put Berndt's life at risk until we know more about the forces we're playing around with . . . "

"You're all cowards," Clubman hissed. "If there had been people like you around in the past we'd have never progressed beyond the wheel!" With a snarl he stormed out of the room.

"He's an angry man," remarked Berndt. He initiated the project. The tachyon accelerator has been his life's work."

"We have a duty to be responsible, Berndt," Christine said. " Now let's get back to the Doctor and his friend."

But when they returned to the laboratory the Doctor and Mel had gone.

"So what was all that about?" asked Mel as they trudged back through the mud and rain to the TARDIS.

"Aha!" said the Doctor cryptically, and opened the police box door for her. "And it's not over yet . . . "

"So where are we off to now?" she asked skipping through the open double doors and into the console room.

The Doctor took out his pocket watch and consulted it. "1693!" he said and operated the dematerialisation switch on the TARDIS console.

Back at the institute, Clubman looked at his watch: it was 4.00am, and the research institute was deathly still. Silently he slipped into the laboratory, and viewed the tachyon accelerator. His crowning achievement, the project he had been working on ever since his days as a young student at university. His every hour had been spent on developing it, to the detriment of all else: friendships, security, relationships. And to be thwarted by cowards acting on the advice of a little man like the Doctor!

The look that Doctor had given him - almost forbidding him to use the accelerator! Forbidding him – Clubman! – to operate his own machine. Well, Christine and Lehmann might listen to the little man's prattlings, but not him!

Determinedly Clubman crossed over to the controls of the tachyon accelerator. The chamber behind the plate-glass window was bathed in an eerie blue light, as tachyon energies shot out and coalesced from the energy panels which lined each of the four walls. Clubman took a deep breath and entered the chamber; the time-energies bathed his body, briefly turning his skin transparent so that his bones and internal organs were visible if there had been anyone to watch.

With a scream of anguish Professor Lionel Clubman vanished from the twenty-first century forever.

Two hours later the compound exploded in a burst of energy as the tachyon accelerator overloaded. There were no casualties, because some ninety minutes previously the head of the security section had received a coded telephone message from an international terrorist group, warning him of a bomb on the premises, and the institute had been speedily evacuated.

The remains of the bomb were never found, and it was assumed that Professor Lionel Clubman had perished in the blast. The only mystery was the identity of the caller, whose voice the security head had described as having a soft Scottish lilt.

"So where are we?" asked Mel as she stepped out of the TARDIS into a sunny wooded glade.

"1693, I told you," said the Doctor.

"Not when," Mel said impatiently. "Where?"

"Harrow Green," said the Doctor and looked around the glade. "The site of what will one day be the research institute."

From nearby there came a sound of groaning. The Doctor and Mel rushed over to the body lying against the trunk of a tree.

"It's Clubman!" gasped Mel, as she recognised the scientist. His face was blazed and scorched. "He used the accelerator and travelled back through time!"

"Who are you?" Clubman croaked through parched lips.

"He doesn't recognise us," said Mel.

"He's delirious," said the Doctor. "His body has been exposed to a massive amount of radiation in the Space/Time Vortex . . . "

"Is he going to die?"

The Doctor shook his head, and took a tub of pills out of his jacket pocket. He forced Clubman to swallow two of the tablets, and placed the tub in Clubman's outstretched hand.

"The tachyon accelerator was a fine piece of equipment," he said to the barely conscious scientist. "But it couldn't protect you from the Time Winds . . . "

"Will he be all right?" asked Mel.

The Doctor looked sadly at Clubman. "He'll be scarred for life I'm afraid. But it will be a long and fruitful life." He stood up. "Come on, we must be off!"

"You can't just leave him here!" protested Mel. "Can't we take him with us? He belongs in the twenty-first century!"

The Doctor grabbed Mel's arm and led her sternly to the TARDIS. "He must stay in the seventeenth century," he insisted and shoved Mel through the open doors of the police box.

As the TARDIS disappeared from 1693 Mel stared angrily at the Doctor, her hands perched on her hips. "I suppose you've got an explanation for what you just did back there?" she demanded.

"I didn't want Doctor Lehmann to use the tachyon accelerator," confessed the Doctor. "That's why I invented that whole load of gobbledegook for Professor Roupie. It would have caused too many temporal anomalies . . . "

"So? Clubman used it to travel back in time." Mel was confused. "The time-lines are still crossed . . . "

The Doctor shook his head.

"Quite the opposite. Clubman travelling back in time was precisely what I wanted to happen," he said. "The accelerator was the culmination of his life's work – I knew he would use it . . . Humans are so predictable." He looked at Mel, with a disappointed look on his face. "You still don't quite understand do you, Mel?"

Mel shook her head.

The Doctor grinned. "Clubman will survive and settle down curiously well in the seventeenth century," he explained. "As time goes by he'll be respected for his great knowledge; he'll even end up becoming a member of the Royal Society."

Mel thought she could see where the Doctor was leading her. "Don't tell me," she said, "There he's responsible for some great scientific breakthrough, without which the twentieth century would never have come about . . . "

"Nothing as mundane as that," said the Doctor. "In two years' time he will marry a delightful young lady named Martha. They will have children and then grandchildren. One of his granddaughters will marry a man named Bush and move to a tiny hamlet called Pease Pottage –"

"Wait a minute – are you saying what I think you're saying?"

The Doctor nodded. "Lionel Clubman is your ancestor – your twelve-times great-grandfather! Without him you would never have been born!"

"And that's why you arranged for him to be sent back in time, with no way of returning," concluded Mel. "Then that means that . . . that . . . "

The Doctor smiled as he adjusted the controls and piloted the TARDIS on to new adventures.

"That's right, Mel. Even before you were born I've just gone and saved your life!"

CROSSWORD ANSWERS

	¹H		²O			³L		⁴M		⁵H		⁶A
⁷R	I	L	L	S		⁸M	U	S	I	C	I	A	N	S
	M		D			N		L		L		O
	⁹A	R	M	S		¹⁰J	A	C	O	N	D	A	N	S
	L		O		¹¹S			C		A		
¹²B	A	T	T	L	E	F	¹³I	E	L	D		
	Y		H		N		K		A		¹⁴M		¹⁵P
¹⁶R	A	C	E		R		¹⁷S	P	O	O	N		¹⁸E	I	R	E
	S		R				E		N		C		I
				¹⁹E	S	C	A	P	E	R	O	U	T	E
	²⁰T		²¹E		P				Y		P		C
²²T	R	E	N	C	H	A	R	²³D		²⁴I	T	C	H
	A		G		E			E			E		A
²⁵W	I	N	I	F	R	E	D			²⁶R	A	R	E
	N		N		E			S			D	

GRIM REALISATION OF A TIME LORD...

TIM QUINN AND DICKY HOWETT

61

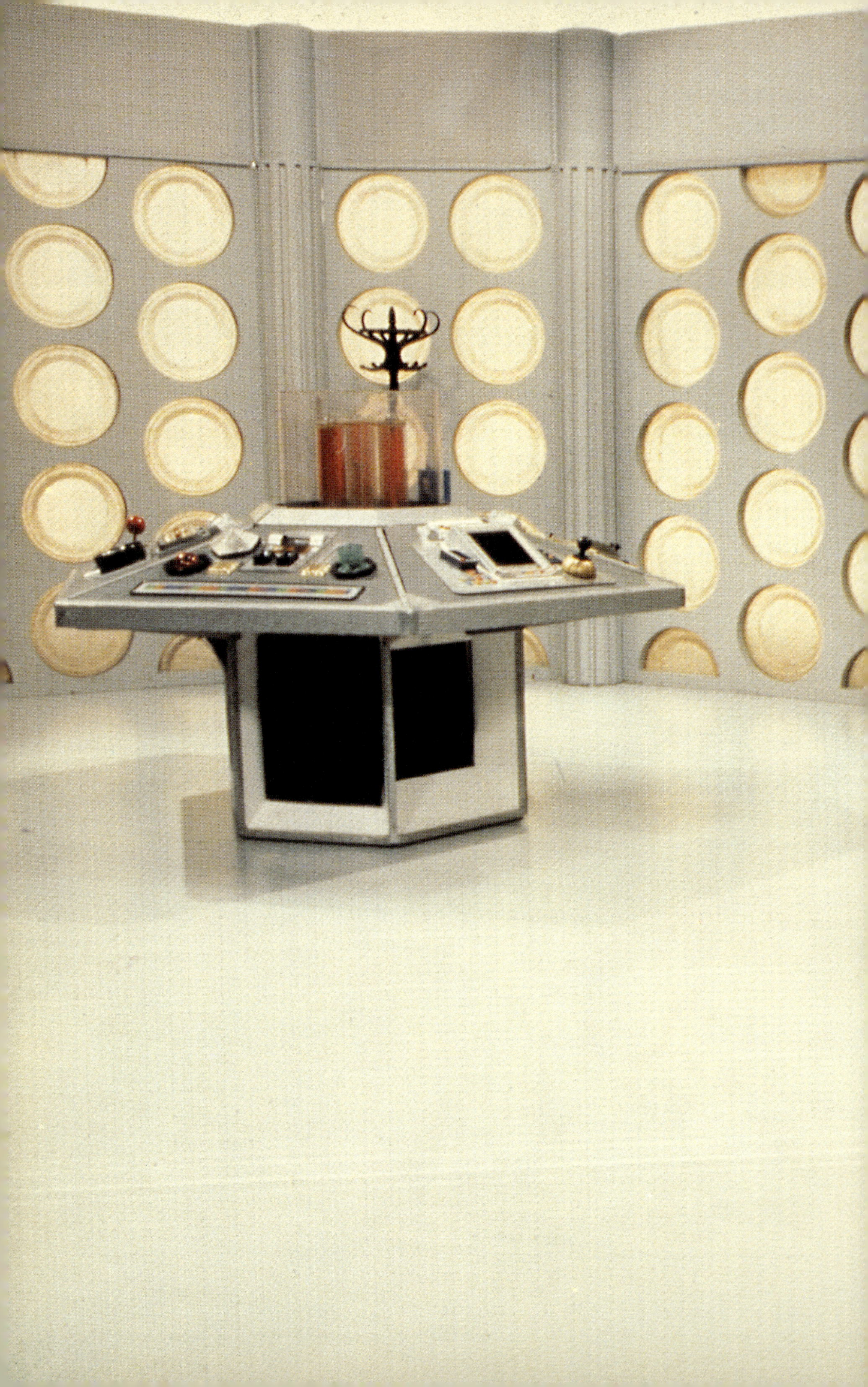